OwnIt!

Own It! Honouring and Amplifying Accountability
Copyright © 2022 by Dr Paige Williams.
All rights reserved.

Published by Grammar Factory Publishing, an imprint of MacMillan Company Limited.

No part of this book may be used or reproduced in any manner whatsoever without the prior written permission of the author, except in the case of brief passages quoted in a book review or article. All enquiries should be made to the author.

Grammar Factory Publishing
MacMillan Company Limited
25 Telegram Mews, 39th Floor, Suite 3906
Toronto, Ontario, Canada
M5V 3Z1

www.grammarfactory.com

Williams, Dr Paige
Own It! Honouring and Amplifying Accountability / Dr Paige Williams.

Paperback ISBN 978-1-98973-758-3
Hardcover ISBN 978-1-98973-760-6
eBook ISBN 978-1-98973-759-0
Audiobook ISBN 978-1-98973-767-5

    1. BUS085000 BUSINESS & ECONOMICS / Organizational Behavior. 2. BUS071000 BUSINESS & ECONOMICS / Leadership. 3. BUS030000 BUSINESS & ECONOMICS / Human Resources & Personnel Management.

Production Credits
Cover design by Designerbility
Interior layout design by Dania Zafar
Book production and editorial services by Grammar Factory Publishing

Grammar Factory's Carbon Neutral Publishing Commitment
From January 1st, 2020 onwards, Grammar Factory Publishing is proud to be neutralizing the carbon footprint of all printed copies of its authors' books printed by or ordered directly through Grammar Factory or its affiliated companies through the purchase of Gold Standard-Certified International Offsets.

Disclaimer
The material in this publication is of the nature of general comment only and does not represent professional advice. It is not intended to provide specific guidance for particular circumstances, and it should not be relied on as the basis for any decision to take action or not take action on any matter which it covers. Readers should obtain professional advice where appropriate, before making any such decision. To the maximum extent permitted by law, the author and publisher disclaim all responsibility and liability to any person, arising directly or indirectly from any person taking or not taking action based on the information in this publication.

OwnIt!

Honouring and Amplifying Accountability

Dr PAIGE WILLIAMS

WHAT PEOPLE ARE SAYING ABOUT OWN IT! ...

In her refreshing new book, *Own It!*, Paige restores integrity and accountability to their proper place at the center of the performance conversation. Through a compelling blend of real-life stories and cutting-edge research, she unlocks the power in the timeless wisdom: say what you'll do and do what you say, and delivers a practical guide for building an accountability culture that enhances individual performance and brings out the best in others.

Own It! is an antidote for the helplessness, spin, and frustration holding back far too many organizations, and is a must read for any leader interested in building more authentic, happier lives for both themselves and their teams.

ANDREW D'ANNA
MANAGING DIRECTOR, CHARLES SCHWAB & CO., INC.

Accountability is a word that is used often, but is often used without understanding exactly what accountability is. In *Own It!*, Dr Paige Williams identifies what it means to be and to call others to account.

There are key challenges in accountability. Paige outlines and explains what these are and suggests the pathway as we journey to greater understanding of what accountability is.

Accountability is not easy, in fact it is hard. But without it, and an accountable culture, the chance of sustained success is unlikely. Whether it be from a professional or personal viewpoint, *Own It!* is a book that will enlighten, inform and lead you to greater accountability.

STEVE HOCKING
CEO GEELONG FOOTBALL CLUB

Owning it is a way of life and Paige is the living embodiment of this truth. In *Own It!* she invites each of us to take responsibility for who we are and what we do with our time at work, in life and on the planet.

MATT CHURCH
FOUNDER, THOUGHT LEADERS

In *Own it!*, Paige has delivered an exceptionally practical and insightful book on how to understand, build and maintain accountability for yourself and others in the workplace. An engaging read, that brings Paige's insights developed through her professional experiences working with leaders across many industries to life, in a clear and accessible format that will benefit many people and organisations.

DREW BESWICK
CEO, POSSABILITY

This book is like wearing contact lenses for the first time – suddenly seeing so clearly, is a shock. *Own It!* cuts through the baffling confusion and craziness we see all around us – in politics, government, sport, even in our private lives, and argues much of it comes from a lack of accountability: we're in an accountability crisis. People don't do what they say they will (or don't admit what they can't), so we all waste time, waste effort, and get demoralised and tired.

Dr Paige Williams draws the sting of accountability, which sounds demanding – and is – by bringing in research that the key to any effective communication, particularly the most challenging level of holding people to account, is relationship – or, as she puts it, love. For Paige, doing what you say; saying what you can't; and being deeply honest with others – and yourself – is integrity in action. With that completely different perspective, it suddenly becomes much easier, not just to understand a great deal of the incompetence and frustration around us, but to do something about it.

This is a brave book. But these are fragile times, and we need brave books. I have coached and taught leaders from around the world for almost thirty years, and books like this, which open up a whole new territory, with both heavyweight science and beautiful writing, come along very rarely. The message is clear and strong and might not be easy for some to hear – but Paige guides us through. It has made a real difference to me, and I warmly recommend it.

ANNE SCOULAR, AUTHOR OF **THE FINANCIAL TIMES GUIDE TO BUSINESS COACHING**,
AND 2020 CO-WINNER OF THE HARVARD BUSINESS REVIEW WARREN BENNIS PRIZE.

Paige has nailed a very important lever not just for performance but for personal success and happiness. Her insights, wisdom and practical perspectives on accountability are backed by significant and cutting-edge research that makes perfect sense for individuals and organisations who want to thrive in a new now.

GARRY THOMPSON
CEO UPLIFTING AUSTRALIA

I had the pleasure of working with Paige as she delivered a bespoke program based on *Own It!* to reset accountability and reduce waste, create connections and boost progress and performance. Paige's well-researched frameworks and incredibly practical and engaging delivery created immediate insight and impact.

I highly recommend *Own It!* to all in leadership positions. I often find myself channelling Paige by remembering every time I point my figure at someone else there are three of my own fingers pointing back at me...

MARK VALENA
FORMER CEO GMHBA, NON-EXECUTIVE DIRECTOR

In *Own It!*, Paige tackles the chunky challenge of accountability and shows ways in which a leader and team can excel in this regard. I have always believed accountability to be an essential element of leadership and this book captures the issue as well as bringing many solutions that any manager/leader can use to enhance their team. I particularly like the concept of creating an accountability system within the team where all can clearly see what they are required to do to ensure the accountability of the team. And of course, the chapter on the *Own It!* mindset brings everything together with frameworks that should be in every leader's kitbag.

GEOFF STALLEY
CHAIR, UPLIFTING AUSTRALIA

CONTENTS

Introduction	1
PART I: *WHY* WE SUCK AT ACCOUNTABILITY	**7**
1. The Other Epidemic	11
2. Wired for Avoidance	25
PART II: *WHAT* WE NEED TO DO TO FIX IT	**39**
3. From Holding to Calling: Resetting Accountability	41
4. Creating Clarity of Accountability Expectations	55
5. Cultivating Quality of Accountability Relationships	77
Part II Wrap-up: The Accountability Reset Matrix	**91**
PART III: *HOW* WE CAN BE BETTER AT IT	**97**
6. Do You Own It? Developing the Right Mindset	103
7. Can You Coach It? (Part 1)	119
8. Can You Coach It? (Part 2)	135
9. Will You Craft It? Shaping a Culture of Accountability	157
Conclusion: Avoiding the 'Dark Side' of Accountability	**179**
Appendix: Case Studies	**185**
Glossary	**199**

ABOUT THE AUTHOR

Dr Paige Williams is an organisational psychologist, executive coach, researcher and author. A PhD in Organisational Behaviour, an Honorary Fellow of the Centre for Wellbeing Science and an Associate of Melbourne Business School, Paige is known as a leadership and culture expert. The potent combination of real-life leadership experience and deep academic knowledge fuels Paige's 'superpower' of translating complex ideas and academic research into real, relevant and relatable solutions for the work that leaders do every day.

Drawing from research in wellbeing, neuroscience, leadership and systems, as well as her own twenty-plus years of international business leadership experience, Paige helps successful leaders – from emerging high potentials to established CEOs – lead themselves, their teams and their organisations to thrive in the dynamic, complex and uncertain environments in which they operate. The results are dramatic and measurable.

Paige has worked with thousands of leaders across business, government, NGOs and education, including the Department of Defence, Charles Schwab, Specsavers, Sawary Energy, Swisse, Maroondah City Council, the Magistrates Court of Victoria, the Transport Accident Commission and The University of Melbourne.

Her first book, *Becoming Antifragile: Learning to Thrive Through Disruption, Challenge and Change*, was published in 2020, and her work has been featured in a variety of academic and non-academic journals, including *Psychology Today*, *Smart Company*, *Australian Financial Review*, and *Human Resource Management*. She presents at conferences internationally and has been interviewed for a variety of media, including national television and radio.

GRATITUDE AND APPRECIATION

My experience of writing this book was like having a second child – you know what's coming, which makes it both easier and harder. I sweated the small stuff less and trusted the process more, but in the same way that it takes a village to raise a child, it is more than just my effort and energy that have breathed life and form into *Own It!*

Thank you to Kelly Irving, who kept me on track with structure, scope and time, and was both gentle and ferocious in her feedback – the perfect combination for a book coach!

To Scott MacMillan, editors Andrew Tracy and Carolyn Jackson, and the whole team at Grammar Factory, thank you for making the production and publishing of this book such a joyful and easy process.

To Matt Church, Lisa O'Neill and the Thought Leaders Business School tribe – thank you for inspiring, encouraging and holding space as I navigated some tough times during the research and writing of this book. You may not have known it, but you were a lifeline in the dark.

I've been blessed to draw on the wisdom and expertise of many wonderful academics and practitioners as I've developed and evolved my thinking around honour and accountability. To my fellow Lab Leaders at MMcQ – Dr Michelle McQuaid, Michelle Etheve and Danielle Jacobs – thank you for your friendship, support, and the many thought-provoking discussions we've had about accountability. They shaped my earliest thinking, and are very present in the chapters on mindset and coaching.

Thank you to Andrew D'Anna, Kane Leersen, Luke Mathers and Glenn Flood for reading early versions of the chapters and sharing your thoughts. To my wise and clever friend Anne Scoular, thank you for our stimulating conversations that helped me understand that it was honour and integrity that underpinned my passion to reset accountability. And thanks as well to my wonderful mentor Lesley Klue, who has helped me find my truth and speak it clearly into the world; I am so grateful for you.

To my practice team – my business manager Nikita Flood, and Cath O'Connell at Wholehearted Marketing – my gratitude for your patience and good humour as we brought to life the ideas in my head. Appreciate you both.

And finally, to my home team – my mum, Margaret, and 'The Angels', my daughters Liv and Pixie. You have had the lived experience of 'honouring and amplifying accountability', as I've written this book. Thank you for being my biggest cheerleaders and for keeping me grounded with love and laughter throughout this journey. I love you.

INTRODUCTION

MAYBE YOU KNOW THERE'S A PROBLEM WITH ACCOUNTABILITY, but you're not confident you know what to do about it.

Maybe you know there's a problem, you know what to do, but you know it won't be easy, so the motivation just isn't there.

Or maybe you know there's a problem, you know what to do *and* feel able to do it, but you're not convinced that you will be supported on the other side.

Accountability affects us all. Whether you're giving or receiving it and whether you need a boost of confidence, motivation or support, I want you to know that *Own It!* will help.

WHY THIS BOOK, NOW?

The thing with writing a book is that the ideas become deeply embedded in your way of thinking, being and doing. It becomes an inherent part of your world view – at least for a while, until that evolves and develops.

In my first book, *Becoming Antifragile: Learning to Thrive Through Disruption, Challenge and Change*, I wrote about our need to remove what's making and keeping us fragile as one of the first steps to becoming more antifragile. Because without addressing the fragility in the first place, there will always be a ceiling to how antifragile we can become.

As I started to look at my own fragility and that of my family, friends, clients and colleagues, there was a common theme in what was holding us back: issues with accountability. Whether that was personal accountability by acknowledging what's ours to own, collective accountability in calling out unacceptable behaviour or practices, or asking others to step into their accountability, this was the thing that was making and keeping us fragile.

But there are layers to this fragility.

I've seen time and again that we don't really know how to 'do' accountability – either with ourselves, or with others. We all have accountability expectations every day. These expectations are so deeply embedded in our social structures that we barely give them a thought, and maybe that's the issue – we aren't conscious and aware of what's going on with these accountability expectations. As a result, we're also not intentional and focused about how we meet or navigate them, which leads to underperformance in both our professional and our personal lives.

Underperformance is an interesting term, so let's pause for a moment to explore what I mean by it. If performance is about meeting or achieving expectations or requirements, and 'high performance' means that we exceed those expectations or requirements, then 'underperformance' means we don't meet them in some way. We don't meet the KPI, support the culture, create safe and effective relationships, live our lives in a meaningful and fulfilling way. And the thing I've observed and experienced about underperformance that's caused by issues with accountability, is that it is *avoidable*. More often than not, there is capacity, motivation and a desire to do better, but the fog of accountability issues prevents them from shining through.

So what does this look like?

In our work, it looks like waste: wasted time, wasted effort, and wasted energy, which then impacts creativity, connection, innovation, productivity, progress and performance.

INTRODUCTION

In our home life, it looks like drama: we create unnecessary struggles for ourselves, we create conflict that could be avoided, and we create suffering that is preventable.

So at one level, this book matters because I've seen so much evidence of how poor we are at 'doing' accountability and the fragility this creates for us personally and professionally.

But as I immersed myself in the research for this book, and as the ideas became embedded in my ways of thinking, being and doing, I realised there was something deeper that accountability means to me.

And that is *honour*.

Accountability is about personal ownership. Accountability is about integrity in action. Accountability is about doing what you say, saying what you'll do – and, perhaps more importantly, what you *can't*. It's about speaking truth and being deeply honest with yourself and others.

Because this is the challenge that I've seen – maybe you have too. Accountability slips sneakily and creeps stealthily. It doesn't exit stage left with a fanfare, oh no: it catches us when we are tired, busy and distracted; when the follow-up conversation feels too hard and it's easier to give someone the benefit of the doubt, 'just this once'. Rarely do we jump off an accountability cliff: like an eroding rock face, accountability slips over time, as we let expectations of ourselves and others slide. And when it does, other important things slip too – things like encouraging inclusive behaviours, hearing diverse perspectives, calling out toxic culture, and modelling human-centred leadership.

So this book is about more than productivity, and will result in more than accelerating progress and improving performance. It is an invitation to return to integrity and honour – an invitation that requires truth and honesty, vulnerability and strength, love and the courage to commit.

Because, when it's done from that place, accountability is an act of *love*. When we call ourselves and others to account from a place of integrity and honour, we are saying, 'I see the greatness in you. You can play a bigger game.'

WHAT'S AHEAD...

In Part I of *Own It!* we explore why accountability is important and why it is an issue. Chapter 1 looks at how accountability is the 'glue in the flat pack' of society; unpacks the three problems that have given accountability such a bad name; and examines how these are fuelling an epidemic of underperformance. In Chapter 2 we examine why accountability is so problematic through the lenses of neuroscience and psychology, and discover some useful ways to help us counter our natural response to take the easy way out.

In Part II, we delve into the antidote to our current epidemic of underperformance. Chapter 3 examines how a fundamental reset of accountability is needed, and what that looks like. Chapters 4 and 5 dive deeper into the two factors that my research determined to be critical in putting that reset into action. Part II wraps up with an invitation for you to assess where you're currently at in terms of your accountability relationships.

In Part III, we move into action as we describe what you can do to reset accountability – firstly with yourself through an Own It! mindset (Chapter 6), then with other people through setting up accountability for success (Chapter 7) and redirecting it when things go wrong (Chapter 8), and finally by creating an Own It! culture within your team or organisation (Chapter 9).

Finally, acknowledging the reality that accountability can be tricky and challenging, we conclude the book by looking at some cautions and caveats, and how best to maintain and sustain this work. The Appendix includes three case studies that explore specific contextual challenges that can tip accountability into the 'dark side'.

INTRODUCTION

Accountability is a fundamental part of the social contract that we engage with every day as we go about our lives. To reset it requires a term that I don't like to use: a paradigm shift. It will ask you to look at the truth of how you are showing up in your personal accountability, how you are asking others to step into theirs, and how you are creating a context in which accountability can thrive.

It is not easy work.

It is not for everyone.

So, with that said, and from a place of love…

I see the greatness in you.
Are you ready to play a bigger game?

PART I

WHY WE SUCK AT ACCOUNTABILITY

Southern Italy, August 1996.
I'm twenty-five years old and managing a 200-bed hotel on the beautiful Amalfi Coast in Italy for a high-end UK tour operator.

We are in the midst of peak season, at full occupancy with busy childcare, water sports and activities programs in full swing. The season is going well but for one thing: we only have 70% of our full allocation of kitchen staff.

The head chef – experienced and in his forties – is struggling under the pressure, and his young team are feeling it too. On this particular morning, the restaurant manager asks to see me and tells me that he's pretty sure that one of the sous chefs is taking wine from the restaurant for his personal consumption. After investigating, the evidence is clear – he's definitely stealing.

I speak with the head chef, who is reluctant for me to take immediate action. The sous chef is a big personality and popular with the kitchen crew – there's no doubt he's helped keep spirits up as the pressure has increased in the last few weeks. To lose another chef at this time could well tip the kitchen team over the edge and impact the service we can provide to our guests. Maybe, he suggests, I could keep the sous chef for a few weeks while we line up a replacement from the UK, and then dismiss him...?

*But now that I know about it (and it's likely others do too), how can I **not** do something?*

Is my responsibility to our guests to deliver a great holiday experience?

Is my responsibility to my organisation, as the point person for the company that the sous chef is stealing from?

Or is my responsibility to my team, to show them that there are clear boundaries that have been crossed?

And what if I sack him and then he fights it - will the company back my decision?

Maybe this is just an accepted behaviour that no one talks about?

AS THE STORY ABOVE MAKES CLEAR, THERE'S NO DOUBT THAT accountability can be a tricky thing.

The implications of calling people to account and letting the consequences of their actions unfold can be significant and wide-reaching. It's understandable that we often choose to turn away from the hard work of it.

The thing is, the implications of turning away are also significant and wide-reaching.

And that's why we need to reset how we think about accountability – to understand and engage with it from a completely different perspective so that it is easier to do with ourselves and with others.

INTRODUCTION

The next couple of chapters will help you to do just that.

In Chapter 1, we dive deeper into the impact that accountability issues have in organisations, and why resetting accountability is the strategic imperative for us to create the positive, purposeful progress we need to succeed in a COVID-impacted operating environment. We also examine the three problems I see that are fuelling the current situation with accountability, and the shift in perspective we need to make in order to address them.

In Chapter 2, we do some root-cause analysis with our accountability issues by looking at how the way our brains are wired and specific psychological processes and perspectives that influence how we react and respond to accountability situations and scenarios.

1.

THE OTHER EPIDEMIC

ACTIVITY BUT NO PROGRESS, MEETINGS WITH NO FOLLOW UP, CONfused responsibilities, impossible demands, missed milestones, low morale, poor engagement, talent drain – there's an epidemic of underperformance in organisations today, and it's being driven by issues with accountability.

From broken promises and unrealistic expectations to finger-pointing and cultures of avoidance and blame, accountability issues – and the fear that drives them – are rampant across business, government, NGOs and beyond.

Do any of these sound familiar?

- You're struggling with a lack of time, too many commitments and a culture of blame.
- You're fed up with being the only one who sees things through and takes personal ownership.
- You've been let down by a broken promise or expected to do the impossible at work.
- You're tired, frustrated and overwhelmed with what lies ahead and can't see a way forward.
- You're a leader who knows your team could perform better, but isn't sure what's holding them back.

Simply put, if you have people in your organisation, you have issues with accountability. And that's a problem, because as the challenges and opportunities of the post-COVID landscape continue to unfold, so does the need to perform.

Sustaining engagement and holding on to talent has always been important, but it is emerging as *the* strategic imperative that will provide the progress and high performance needed for organisations to survive and thrive in our new economic context, in which workers are reassessing what 'good work' and a 'good life' look like.

> **Let's say that one more time:**
>
> *Accountability is the strategic imperative in the post-COVID economic landscape.*

Why is this?

Because without accountability, nothing sticks: not your latest transformational change initiative, not your best talent, nothing.

Without accountability, poor-quality work, decisions and leadership go unchallenged, and 'ethical slip' starts to happen.

Without accountability, leaders, teams and organisations fall behind as the scale of disruption, complexity of change, and pace of technological advancement increase.

Without accountability, we waste time, money and energy in a fog of confusion and dysfunctional, ineffective accountability relationships.

From my twenty-plus years as a senior leader and my work with the CEOs, senior executives and leaders who are my clients, I know that accountability underpins success. And multiple research studies agree.

In fact, research suggests that when organisations get accountability wrong:

- 75% of team members see solving problems as 'someone else's job',
- 65% don't see due dates as real commitments,
- 80% don't seek and offer feedback often,
- 82% try but fail to hold others accountable (or avoid it altogether), and
- 85% are unsure what the organisation is trying to achieve.

When we get accountability wrong, poor results, failed initiatives, missed targets, low morale and engagement, and an environment with more blame than trust follow.

Things get worse without anyone knowing why or accepting the accountability to do something about it. The result is pervasive fragility that shows up as anxiety, stress and underperformance in both professional and personal contexts – an epidemic that spreads across all layers and levels of society as we lose touch with honour and integrity, and traditional approaches to leadership fail us.

And if we weren't good at it before (and let's face it, most of us weren't), the added complexity of COVID and its impact on employees, team structures and ways of working have made accountability feel even harder.

Accountability issues keep us fragile to disruption and uncertainty.

SO, WHAT'S THE PROBLEM?

When I talk to leaders around the world, I'm hearing things like:

- 'It feels harder to lead a hybrid and distributed workforce – it takes more time, effort and energy.'

- 'My people's priorities and expectations of work and life have changed – what was okay before is less okay now.'
- 'Accountability conversations can be tricky at the best of times – they're even harder when they're in a virtual environment.'

Unfortunately, team members are seeing leaders' lack of action on accountability very differently. This is what I'm hearing from the teams I'm working with:

- 'We have this "culture of politeness" where no one talks about the real issues. We all know there are problems, but there seems to be this understanding that no one calls them out. How can I start when no one else is?'
- 'It's so frustrating that 20% of the people do 80% of the work and no one does anything about it. I'm being asked to do more and more, but I see others doing less and less. How can they get away with it? Why isn't management holding them accountable for their responsibilities?'
- 'It's just confusing and demoralising. We spend so much time talking in meetings, but very few action points come out of it and even if they do, no one follows up, so most of them don't get done anyway. I mean really, what's the point?'

Part of the problem is that accountability is so deeply embedded in the way we live, work and play that we don't even see it. This is because accountability is universal: it's the oil in the engine of human interaction. Imagine if you could not rely on *anyone* to do *anything* they said they would or were expected to do – it's not hard to see how quickly chaos follows in that scenario. Without accountability, coordinated activities become difficult at best, and impossible at worst.

Accountability is also a requisite for social order: it is the glue that binds social systems together. Imagine what would happen if we didn't have accountability to shared expectations. Travel timetables become meaningless, stop signs irrelevant… and visiting a doctor? Well, that depends on whether they decide to show up today. Despite the fact it's so deeply embedded that we don't notice it most of the time, accountability is what enables the systems of our societies and the structures of social order to operate successfully.

Accountability is the oil in the wheels, the glue in the social systems, and the angel on the shoulder of each of us. When it's missing, progress slows, instability grows, and bad stuff happens.

And accountability has a moral imperative too: it is the angel on our shoulder. Imagine if individuals could act without regard to the consequences of their actions. It is comforting to think that people would do the right thing even without consequences, but in reality that isn't the case. As Adam Smith so wisely said in his 1759 book *The Theory of Moral Sentiments*, 'A moral being is an accountable being.'

THE 3 ISSUES WE NEED TO ADDRESS

There are three critical issues that we need to address to make progress with accountability:

- *Confusion* in understanding,
- *Concern* in application, and
- *Contexts* that undermine.

Let's examine each of these in detail.

1. Confusion

Accountability is complex, fuzzy and confusing. One of the biggest challenges is that it means different things to different people – often in the same organisation, and even in the same team. This leads to what has been called 'multiple accountabilities disorder'.

Part of the issue is that there is a popular fallacy in organisations that holding people accountable for their actions is an effective means to control behavioural outcomes. However, research shows that accountability-inducing practices are not uniformly effective, because the way they are understood and adopted varies by individual. I'm sure we've all experienced scenarios in which team members have been exposed to the same situation, but hold quite different expectations about their accountability within it. This discrepancy exists because individual interpretations of external situations and systems are subjective, and so differ from person to person.

Added to this is a time-related factor. The subjective experience of *being accountable* is different from the subjective *retrospective evaluation of accountability* that takes place after the event in traditional approaches to accountability, such as performance reviews.

And to top it all off, there's a problem with language, as words like 'accountability', 'responsibility' and 'ownership' are so often used interchangeably. Combine this with the wild variances of subjective individual interpretation, and it's not surprising that there's so much confusion about what accountability really means and looks like.

How consistent is the understanding of accountability in your organisation or your team?

2. Concern

Accountability is often only asked for once things have gone wrong – the conversations come too late, people are defensive, and so it can feel hard to do them well.

If I were to invite you to a meeting so that we could have an accountability conversation, my guess is that it wouldn't be top on your list of 'favourite things to do today'. And that's because accountability has had a bad rap; if it were an A-list celebrity, accountability would need to fire its agent!

We use accountability as a stick to 'punish' people when situations have gone wrong. It's often reactive, and usually comes when the situation is no longer retrievable – the classic move of shutting the stable door after the horse has bolted. Unfortunately, too often 'holding people to account' is done from a place of wanting to name, shame and apportion blame. Just the language we use tells a lot about the motivation and energy of the action.

How confident do you feel having accountability conversations? Because of this, accountability conversations feel punitive; it's like we're telling someone off and pointing out what they've not done, where they've not delivered, and, ultimately, how they're not good enough. And usually, this is done at a time when it's too late for them to do anything about it anyway. Is it any wonder these conversations are met with defensiveness, and feel so hard to do?

3. Context

When it comes to accountability, context matters. A variety of 'macro' factors, such as team culture, conflicting pressures, multiple demands, and the specific characteristics of sources of accountability can positively or negatively influence individual accountability.

The problem is that because it feels so uncomfortable, leaders are unsure how to embed accountability into the culture of their teams and the organisation so that it becomes a normal part of how work gets done.

Is accountability part of your team culture? Added to this, employees often face numerous, conflicting accountability requirements through matrix reporting structures and multiple strategic agendas. Public administration research has found that such conflicts lead to poor decision-making and performance.

These three issues – confusion, concern and context – are why we need to create a new understanding of accountability that moves it from a means to punish people to a tool that can set us up for success. This reset of accountability requires a shift in mindsets, attitudes and behaviours so that we can confidently role model, coach, and create contexts and cultures that support accountability.

The good news is that resetting accountability doesn't have to be difficult, expensive or time-consuming. Small shifts in mindsets, attitudes, and leader and team practices can have a big impact on accountability, learning, progress and performance.

Here's what we need to do:

1. *We need to let go of the idea that accountability is 'hard', 'tricky', or requires 'courageous' conversations.*

We often hear about the need for 'courageous conversations' in workplaces. Rather than being conversations in which we are vulnerable (the original meaning of the term, as used in Brené Brown's *Dare to Lead*), I find this is often code for accountability conversations. In my experience, when leaders listen to the right voices and coach for accountability, there is a clarity to these discussions that removes the need for them to be 'courageous'.

2. *We need to stop thinking of accountability as a 'nice-to-have' and understand that it is the foundation for higher performance and engagement from both individuals and teams.*

Workplace researcher Cy Wakeman has found that, on average, employees spend two-and-a-half hours each day engaged in workplace drama, of which 23% is due to lack of accountability. Despite many organisations focusing on employee engagement as a key driver for performance, Wakeman's research shows that it is accountability rather than engagement that drives business success (we'll explore this further in Chapter 7).

3. *We each need to recognise and own our role in the current situation and be prepared to 'show up' differently to move it forward.*

Accountability issues don't happen on their own – they are created by people. Whether you are asking for accountability and not receiving what you believe you need, or being asked for it in a way or at a scale that you feel is not appropriate, the first accountability to step into is your role and responsibility in the current situation. What is yours to own?

THE OPPORTUNITY IN RESETTING ACCOUNTABILITY

By resetting accountability, we reduce stress by wasting less time and energy in drama. We save money by creating more-effective work practices. We support higher performance and better-quality work outcomes by enabling forward learning and growth for ourselves and our people. We become clear on the high talent and potential in our teams, and focus our energy on those staff who are engaged in their work and prepared to be called to account.

By owning what is ours to own, we strengthen connection, encourage development, and support purposeful progress and high performance. We move beyond fear to develop fruitful relationships based in trust and confidence, and we create clear expectations that invite people to be their best as they take meaningful and effective action that will benefit themselves, their team, their workplace, and beyond.

SUMMARY

- » We are in the midst of an accountability crisis, which has produced an epidemic of fragility that is showing up as anxiety, stress and underperformance across all layers and levels of society.

- » There are three main issues that need to be addressed:
  - Confusion in understanding
  - Concern in application
  - Contexts that undermine

- » In order to correct these, we need to adjust our thinking so that we understand that:
  - Accountability is not 'hard' or 'tricky', and can be accomplished through clarity rather than 'courage'.
  - Accountability is not a 'nice-to-have', but rather the foundation for higher performance and engagement from both individuals and teams.
  - We must clearly recognise our own role and responsibility in the current situation in order to properly embed accountability in our workplaces.

- » When we reset accountability in our workplace relationships, we reduce stress, save money, support higher performance and better-quality work, and encourage development, resulting in positive, purposeful progress.

FROM IDEAS TO ACTION

- Think about the three accountability issues: *confusion*, *concern* and *context*.
  - » How do each of these play out in your team and/or workplace?
  - » What impact does each of them have on relationships, progress, performance and morale?

- If you could wave a magic wand and reset accountability in your team or workplace, what difference would it make?
  - » How different would it feel to be there?
  - » What would be able to be achieved that isn't possible right now?
  - » What are at least three changes that you can predict as a result of resetting accountability?

References

'Without accountability poor quality work, decisions and leadership go unchallenged and 'ethical slip' starts to happen...' Sinek, S. (2019). *The Infinite Game: How to Lead in the 21st Century*. Random House.

'I know that accountability underpins success. And multiple research studies agree...' The Leaders Lab Workplace Survey 2021, Workplace Accountability Study 2014.

'In fact, research suggests that when organizations get accountability wrong...' The Leaders Lab Workplace Survey 2021, Workplace Accountability Study, 2014.

'It's accountability that enables the systems of our societies and structures of social order to operate successfully...' Hall, A. T., Blass, F. R., Ferris, G. R., & Massengale, R. (2004). Leader reputation and accountability in organizations: Implications for dysfunctional leader behavior. *The Leadership Quarterly*, 15(4), 515-536.

'As Adam Smith so wisely said, "A moral being is an accountable being..."' Adam Smith, *The Theory of Moral Sentiments*, 1754.

'This leads to what has been called 'multiple accountabilities disorder...' Koppell, J. G. (2005). Pathologies of accountability: ICANN and the challenge of "multiple accountabilities disorder". *Public Administration Review*, 65(1), 94-108.

'Research shows that accountability-inducing practices are not uniformly effective because the way they are understood and adopted varies by individual...' Frink, D. D. & Klimoski, R. J. (1998). Toward a theory of accountability in organizations and human resource management. *Research in Personnel and Human Resources Management*, 16, 1-52; Tetlock, P. E. (1985). Accountability: The neglected social context of judgment and choice. *Research in Organizational Behavior*, 7(1), 297-332; Tetlock, P. E. (1992). The impact of accountability on judgment and choice: Toward a social contingency model. *Advances in Experimental Social Psychology*, 25, 331-376.

'Public administration research has found that such conflicts led to poor decision making and performance by team members...' Romzek, B. S. & Dubnick, M. J. (1987). Accountability in the public sector: Lessons from the Challenger tragedy. *Public Administration Review*, 47(3), 227-238.

'In Brené Brown's Dare to Lead...' Brown, B. (2018). *Dare to Lead: Brave Work. Tough Conversations. Whole Hearts.* Random House.

'**Workplace researcher Cy Wakeman has found that on average, employees spend two-and-a-half hours each day in workplace drama, of which 23% is due to lack of accountability**...' Wakeman, C. (2017), *No Ego: How Leaders Can Cut Workplace Drama, End Entitlement and Drive Big Results.* St Martin's. Press.

2.

WIRED FOR AVOIDANCE

'We just need people to be more accountable.'

THIS IS A PHRASE I OFTEN HEAR FROM THE LEADERS I WORK WITH. The problem is, when leaders say this, what their people hear is 'You're not doing enough,' or 'You're letting me down.'

This is because accountability is what gets discussed when things are going wrong, rather than being addressed up front as a means of setting things up for success. It's this punitive view of accountability that holds leaders, teams and organisations back from boosting progress and performance. Because what it triggers is fear.

Fear is primal, and it's powerful. It activates a gamut of processes and reactions in our brains and bodies which have powerful consequences for the way we think, feel and behave. This is why it's useful to understand the neuroscience and psychology of accountability, and how they influence us when we're asking for or being asked for accountability.

Once we have this understanding and awareness, we're able to move away from experiences of avoidance and underperformance filled with frustration and drama, and towards ones of ownership, where we achieve clarity, confidence and learning that fast-tracks progress, performance and success.

FEAR AND THE ACCOUNTABILITY COIN

There are two sides to the accountability coin, and each of them has different fears associated with it.

On one side of the coin is the role of the person asking for accountability – the *Accountor*.

When we are in the role of Accountor, we can feel reluctant to hold people to account for fear of being seen as 'the bad guy' and being disliked. Another risk of taking on this role is becoming the 'odd one out', and finding ourselves isolated in our workplace.

On the other side of the accountability coin is the role of the person being asked for accountability – the *Accountee*.

When we are in the role of Accountee, lack of clarity and commitment to action can make us reluctant to ask what is expected of us for fear we may not be able to deliver. And for those of us who typically take on too much, we may be unwilling to call out unrealistic expectations for fear of losing face, status, or our job.

This fear-based response helps explain why Phillip E. Tetlock, a leading researcher of accountability, has suggested that accountability may be the most pervasive and perhaps most powerful single influence on human behaviour. Taking a closer look at the psychology and neuroscience of accountability can help us understand why the way we're wired makes accountability such a thorny issue.

THE NEUROSCIENCE OF ACCOUNTABILITY

The unfortunate reality is that we are wired for avoidance.

The organising principle of the brain is to 'minimise danger, maximise reward'. It processes every piece of incoming data through this filter and assesses how we should respond in order to manage what neuroscientist Lisa Feldman-Barrett calls our 'body budget'.

Effectively, our brain is constantly asking the question: 'Is the return on investment for this energy expenditure going to be worth it? Is this action going to add value in some way to my existence here and now and help me survive in the future, or not?'

Consequently, in every moment of every day, our brain is assessing and making decisions – most of which are below our level of conscious awareness – about whether this moment is a potential opportunity (an investment in the body budget and our chances of surviving and thriving in the future) or a potential threat (a withdrawal from the budget and a lessening of our chances of surviving and thriving in the future).

When we perceive opportunity, our brain releases a slew of positive neurotransmitters and hormones (serotonin, dopamine, oxytocin) through our brain and body, and we move towards it. When we perceive something as a threat, our brain releases cortisol, the stress hormone that triggers the classic fight-or-flight response, and we move away or avoid it.

But it isn't as simple as what's happening here and now.

Past vs. present

When confronted with something that it perceives as either an opportunity or a threat, your brain draws on your lifetime of past experiences – things that have happened to you personally, as well as things that you've learned from friends, teachers, books, YouTube, TikTok, and so on – and in the blink of an eye reconstructs bits and pieces of past experience, as your neurons pass electrochemical information back and forth in a complex, ever-shifting network. It then assembles these into memories to infer the meaning of the incoming sense data and make a 'best guess' as to what to do about it.

And your past experiences include not only what happened in the world around you, but also what happened *inside* your body. So, based on your physical reactions in the moment, your brain will scan your memory for similar situations in the past that elicited these sensations: for example, 'What other situations made my heart beat quickly?' 'What previous encounters made me breathe this heavily?'

What your brain is essentially asking itself in every moment is, 'When my body was in a similar state, what did I do next?' The answer doesn't need to be a perfect match for your current situation – it just requires something close enough to give your brain an appropriate plan of action that helps you survive and thrive.

You've experienced this many times: when you see a face in a crowd and you think it's someone you know, so you go to say 'Hello'; or when you're out walking in the bush and you see what your brain tells you is a snake, but turns out to be a stick. This is your brain filling in the gaps and jumping to conclusions without all the evidence.

Perception vs. reality

So basically, your brain is a prediction machine – a bit like a crystal ball in your head. Its answer to the question, 'What did I do next when I experienced this before?' becomes your current lived experience. In other words, your brain combines information from outside and inside your head to produce everything you see, hear, smell, taste and feel.

Pretty impressive, huh?

So let's put your prediction machine to the test.

Take a moment and think about your favourite food.
For me, this would be a warm dark chocolate brownie with cold whipped cream.
Imagine its smell…
Its taste…
It texture, how it feels in your mouth…

Are you salivating yet?

If neuroscientists were scanning your brain right now, they might see the regions that are related to the senses of taste and smell, as well as those that control saliva, lighting up like a Christmas tree. And if thinking about your favourite food made your mouth water, then you changed the firing of your own neurons in the same way that the brain's automatic predictions do.

This process is similar to what you interpret when you 'read' an expression on your partner's face or interpret a 'tone' in your boss's voice: your brain interprets, assigns meaning, and takes action based on that perception. And ultimately, in each moment, one prediction is the winner.

All of which is to say, *your brain is not wired for accuracy* – it's wired to keep you safe *in the moment* to better guarantee your future existence. The predictions your brain makes are biased towards this end. And this can be a real problem when it comes to accountability.

UNDERSTANDING YOUR TRIGGERS: THE SCARF MODEL

The SCARF model devised by Dr David Rock is a great tool for understanding what can trigger a threat/avoidance response, and as such is a useful aid for navigating our accountability relationships more successfully. The model suggests that the following five factors can be powerful threat triggers for the brain:

- **Status** – your relative importance to others
- **Certainty** – your ability to predict the future
- **Autonomy** – your perception of control, freedom and choice
- **Relatedness** – your sense of safety, belonging and connection
- **Fairness** – your perception of transparency and justice

Figure 2.1 that follows suggests ways that we can dial down threats and dial up rewards for each of the SCARF factors in the context of accountability relationships in the workplace.

Your brain is wired for safety, and that means it can want to avoid accountability at all costs. Let's see what this could look like in a scenario played out in two ways – one that trips the SCARF trigger points, and another one that doesn't.

Scenario #1

Imagine you're in the role of Accountee. You are working on a project, and your Accountor asks to meet with you. They provide you with no context for the meeting, nor tell you how long you can expect it to go for (*Certainty* trigger).

Their opening question is, 'Can I give you some feedback?' (*Status* trigger). They then follow this up with a list of the things you *should* be doing, instead of what you *are* doing (*Autonomy* trigger).

They provide little opportunity for you to comment (*Fairness* trigger), and rush you out once they've finished telling you what to do because they have a call to make (*Relatedness* trigger).

Can you imagine how you would feel coming out of this conversation? Would you feel confident, motivated and supported to meet the accountability challenges ahead?

No, me neither.

Scenario #2

So now let's imagine you're in the role of Accountor and – understanding how our brains are wired and the SCARF trigger points – you approach the same scenario somewhat differently.

SCARF in Action

Dial Down Threat		Dial Up Reward
Provide strengths-based feedback, show appreciation, reward learning and progress towards goals as well as outcomes.	**Status** — relative importance to others	Provide strengths-based feedback, show appreciation, reward learning and progress towards goals as well as outcomes.
Create plans, strategies and maps. Break complex projects down into smaller steps. Establish clear expectations and desirable outcomes.	**Certainty** — able to predict the near future	Make ideas and assumptions explicit. Provide clear objectives and timeframes.
Provide options and choice over task, time, technique and team where possible.	**Autonomy** — a sense of control, freedom and choice	Provide multiple options for choice such as self-directed learning plans, self-managed workflow and flexibility in working hours.
Use video for remote team meetings to enhance connection and intentionally build social capital.	**Relatedness** — a sense of safety with others	Set up buddy, mentoring or coaching relationships and small action learning groups.
Increase transparency, communication and involvement in decisions impacting the team.	**Fairness** — a perception of transparency and fair exchanges	Set clear ground rules, expectations and objectives and share them with the team.

Figure 2.1: The SCARF model

You ask your Accountee for a catch-up, explaining that you only have thirty minutes before you need to make a call (*Certainty*).

Your opening question to them is, 'I can see you're making progress; how do you feel things are going?' (*Status*). Once you've heard from them, you present the issues that you're concerned about and ask, 'What do you think is the best way for us to address this?' (*Autonomy*).

Having listened to their ideas (*Fairness*) and added your thoughts, you both agree on the next steps, and you bring the discussion to a close a few minutes before time so that you can ask about a non-work-related topic – family, hobby, and so forth (*Relatedness*).

This version of the conversation supports the SCARF factors, and in doing so helps the Accountee to feel confident, motivated and supported to take the necessary next steps to move the project forward.

As these two scenarios demonstrate, by understanding where our neurological 'trip wires' are, we can learn to navigate accountability conversations far more effectively.

THE PSYCHOLOGY OF ACCOUNTABILITY

The neuroscience of accountability provides us with an understanding of the physiological responses that we have to accountability. But as we explored above, it is your brain's ability to predict based on its perception and interpretation of past experiences that drives these responses. It is these interpretation and perception processes that take us from the physiological, brain-based realm of neuroscience to the cognitive, mind-based territory of psychology.

This is why understanding the three psychological perspectives that most frequently come into play in accountability situations helps us understand why people so often have adverse reactions in these situations *and* suggests strategies that allow us to navigate those situations more effectively. These perspectives are as follows:

1. The **Social** perspective suggests that Accountees protect their self-image and look to gain reward and avoid punishment in social groups through favourable evaluations by others. This provides an insight into motivation and the social factors that may trigger a threat/avoidance response.

2. The **Internal** perspective suggests that, because accountability involves the expectation of a potential evaluation, it is driven by the same psychological processes as social identity and approval-seeking. This speaks to the Status aspect of the SCARF model, in that responses are driven by a fear of loss of social status, and helps us understand why Accountees may automatically take a defensive position in accountability situations.

3. The **Phenomenological** perspective proposes that accountability is a 'state of mind' rather than a 'state of affairs'. This puts the focus on the Accountee's subjective interpretations of the accountability situation they are facing, rather than the objective systems or processes of accountability employed by the organisation.

Each of these perspectives will be important as we explore how we can shift away from *holding* people to account to *calling* them to step into their accountability in the chapters ahead.

For the moment, though, I want to reiterate the central truth of this chapter: that all of us, by nature, are wired for avoidance. Once we understand more about how that wiring works, we become more aware of how it influences us when asking for or being asked for accountability.

And with that awareness comes choice: we can *choose* to leave avoidance and underperformance behind, and intentionally move towards ownership, confidence and clarity. Understanding our brain wiring and psychology makes us more effective as both Accountors and Accountees, as it helps us to feel better, perform better, and lead better – both others, and ourselves.

SUMMARY

» Understanding the way our brain is wired and the psychological processes that drives accountability can support us to be more effective as both Accountors and Accountees.

» Our brains are wired to avoid situations that we perceive as threatening and trigger a fear response, which has consequences for accountability.

» The roles of Accountor (asking for accountability) and Accountee (being asked for accountability) trigger different fears:

- As Accountors, we may be unwilling to call people to account for fear of being disliked and isolated.

- As Accountees, we may be scared to ask for clarification about what is expected of us for fear we may not be able to deliver, or be reluctant to call out unrealistic expectations for fear of losing face, status, or our job.

» The organising principle of the brain is to 'minimise danger, maximise reward' in order to manage our 'body budget'.

» The SCARF model identifies five factors that can be powerful threat triggers for the brain:

1. **Status** – your relative importance to others
2. **Certainty** – your ability to predict the future
3. **Autonomy** – your perception of control, freedom and choice
4. **Relatedness** – your sense of safety, belonging and connection
5. **Fairness** – your perception of transparency and justice

» There are three psychological perspectives that can help us to navigate accountability more effectively:

- The **Social** perspective suggests that Accountees protect their self-image and look to gain reward and avoid punishment in social groups through favourable evaluations by others.

- *The **Internal** perspective suggests that because accountability involves the expectation of a potential evaluation by another, which involves a risk to social status, it is driven by less-than-conscious psychological processes that can result in defensive responses.*

- *The **Phenomenological** perspective proposes that accountability is determined more by the subjective perceptions of the Accountee than the objective reality of the accountability situation itself.*

FROM IDEAS TO ACTION

- Think about a current accountability challenge you have as an Accountor.
    - » Which SCARF factor(s) can you see at play in this situation?
    - » What impact is it/are they having?
    - » How could you dial down the threat and/or dial up the rewards for that factor?

- Think about a current accountability challenge you have as an Accountee.
    - » Which SCARF factor(s) can you see at play?
    - » What impact is it/are they having?
    - » How could you dial down the threat and/or dial up the rewards for that factor?

References

'In order to manage what neuroscientist Lisa Feldman-Barrett calls our 'body budget'...' Feldman Barrett, L. (2020). *Seven and a Half Lessons about the Brain*. Picador.

'Dr David Rock's research helps us understand and be aware of...' Rock, D. (2009). *Your Brain at Work: Strategies for Overcoming Distraction, Regaining Focus, and Working Smarter All Day Long*. HarperCollins.

'The Social perspective...' Doherty, K. & Schlenker, B. R. (1991). Self-consciousness and strategic self-presentation. *Journal of Personality, 59*(1), 1-18; Schlenker, B. R., Britt, T. W., Pennington, J., Murphy, R. & Doherty, K. (1994). The triangle model of responsibility. *Psychological Review, 101*(4), 632.

'The Internal perspective...' Tetlock, P. E. (1985). Accountability: The neglected social context of judgment and choice. *Research in Organizational Behavior, 7*(1), 297-332; Tetlock, P. E. (1992). The impact of accountability on judgment and choice: Toward a social contingency model. *Advances in Experimental Social Psychology, 25*, 331-376.

'The Phenomenological perspective...' Tetlock, P. E. (1985). Accountability: The neglected social context of judgment and choice. *Research in Organizational Behavior, 7*(1), 297-332; Tetlock, P. E. (1992). The impact of accountability on judgment and choice: Toward a social contingency model. *Advances in Experimental Social Psychology, 25*, 331-376.

PART II

WHAT WE NEED TO DO TO FIX IT

City of London, 1994.
I'm working as an account executive for Citigate Communications, a financial and corporate PR firm. My two main clients are the fast-food brand KFC and Lucas Industries, a multinational automotive and engineering firm.

These clients couldn't be more different in their marketing communications targets and messaging, but interestingly I'm managing environmental projects for each of them – an Environmental Community Awards program for KFC, and a consumer education campaign to try to neutralise the negative messaging around emissions from diesel engines for Lucas. The clients have different account managers and so I have different reporting lines for each project – and they are about as different in nature as the clients themselves!

Having run the awards program herself for many years, my KFC account manager took me through an overview of the program timing and critical milestones at a kick-off meeting. I know what aspects of the work I'm responsible for and when I need to complete them so that we can deliver *on our promise to the client. We meet on a weekly basis to check in on progress and talk though any challenges so that she can provide the clarity or support I may need to keep the work progressing.*

My Lucas account manager – not so much. There was no kick-off meeting to begin the campaign, I'm unclear as to my responsibilities, and we meet on an almost daily basis to go over the work I'm doing. She talks about the 'buck stopping with her' with the client, but doesn't seem to want to share the responsibility of developing and delivering the campaign. Timing and priorities often shift, and she insists on seeing a draft of every email I send to the client before it goes out – despite me having worked on the account for over a year.

I'm feeling frustrated, and have lost confidence in my ability to know what needs to be done or to do the work well.

IN PART I, WE LOOKED AT THE EPIDEMIC OF UNDERPERFORMANCE that's being driven by issues with accountability, and how an understanding of our psychological processes and the way our brains are wired can help us navigate these issues more successfully. We're now going to explore why, in order to make purposeful progress and succeed, we need to 'reset' accountability, and the two critical factors that can help us do just that.

In Chapter 3, we look at how we can liberate accountability from the shocking PR it's been given and reset it from *holding* people to account from a place of power and control to *calling* them to it from a place of love and trust.

Chapters 4 and 5 explore the two factors that my research found can make the difference in doing this reset: the *clarity of accountability expectations* and the *quality of accountability relationships*.

3.

FROM HOLDING TO CALLING: RESETTING ACCOUNTABILITY

RESETTING ACCOUNTABILITY IS PARTICULARLY RELEVANT FOR TEAMS and organisations right now, because in disruptive and ambiguous environments there are often more unknowns than knowns, and many of the challenges we face do not have clear solutions.

Leadership experts Ron Heifetz and Marty Linsky refer to these kinds of challenges as 'adaptive'.

Adaptive challenges are situations in which:

- The problem is difficult to clearly define, and to do so may require adopting new perspectives – which means that,
- The solution is currently unknown, will definitely require learning new methods and perhaps evaluating new values – and therefore,
- This work needs to be achieved through innovation and influence rather than authority and power.

Heifetz and Linsky contrast these types of challenges with 'technical challenges', which are problems that can be solved by the existing knowledge of experts and achieved through the exercise of authority and power. When facing a technical challenge, it's more a case of 'doing the admin' – working through the process and completing the necessary tasks that will rectify the situation – whereas in the case of an adaptive challenge, it is less a matter of finding the right 'fix' than of re-examining and re-evaluating our whole approach to the problem.

The COVID pandemic gives us a particularly stark example of the distinction between these challenges: producing a vaccine was primarily a technical challenge, and one that was accomplished with relative speed; getting people to *take* the vaccine, on the other hand, has proven to be a far more complex, adaptive challenge.

So, what does this have to do with accountability?

Well, in my experience, issues with accountability can cause technical problems – ones whose solutions should be fairly straightforward – to become or at the very least *feel like* adaptive ones, because the 'fog' of accountability issues means that there is little clarity over who is doing what, when, why or with whom, let alone an understanding of how it all fits into the bigger picture and the consequences if we don't deliver.

In Chapter 1, we talked about three major problems that often arise in accountability situations – *confusion*, *concern* and *context* – which make conversations about accountability about as welcome as a fox in a chicken pen for most people.

The central issue here is that, too often, we *hold* people to account from a place of power and control. Much like we might hold up a bank or a corner store: we storm in, waving our accountability processes and systems around like weapons, looking to scare everyone into submission. Alternatively, we may take a more passive-aggressive 'punitive judgement' approach, in which, armed with our pointy 'should' finger, we name, blame and shame. (And it's not only others who get that finger pointed at them: as we'll discover in Chapter 6 when we explore the central importance of *mindset* to accountability, we can just as often turn the blame upon ourselves.)

In both of these scenarios, accountability is weaponised and used as a form of discipline. We are made to pay for our missteps and mistakes after they have been made, and often when there is little opportunity to do anything about it.

When we *hold* people (including ourselves) to account in this manner, it is based on a dominator power dynamic and the energy of fear. The best we can hope to achieve with this is compliance – but that compliance is obtained at the cost of people retreating into smaller and smaller spaces where they can feel safe and settling for underperformance for fear of risking failure.

This is about as far away as possible from the courageous creativity and inspiring innovation we need to meet the challenges and leverage the opportunities in the uncertain and complex environments in which we, our teams and our organisations operate.

But what if there was a different way?

What if, rather than *holding* people to account, we *called* them there?

What if, rather than being used as a post-facto punishment for missteps and mistakes, accountability set us up for success right from the beginning?

What if, rather than being driven by fear, accountability became an act of love?

I know, I know – it sounds like a stretch, doesn't it?

But if we're going to be better at accountability (and we need to be), this is where we need to go. And a good place to start is by having a deeper understanding of exactly what accountability is and how it 'works'.

GETTING TO KNOW ACCOUNTABILITY: EXPLANATION–EVALUATION–CONSEQUENCES

If a squirrel is only a rat with a fluffy tail, better branding and a good agent, then accountability is just the rat. It's had such a raw deal on the PR and brand-image front that it needs to have its reputation rebuilt from the ground up. And the best place to start is with a definition of what it actually is.

In the academic literature, accountability is defined as 'a perceived expectation that one's decisions or actions will be evaluated by a salient audience and that rewards or sanctions are believed to be contingent on this expected evaluation'.

Using this definition, we can identify three critical elements of accountability:

1. An **Explanation** from the Accountor of the responsibilities that the Accountee is accountable for;

2. an **Evaluation** by the Accountor of the Accountee's fulfilment of those responsibilities; and finally,

3. the **Consequences** of that evaluation for the Accountee, whether positive or negative.

And, just like a three-legged stool, if one of these elements is missing, accountability collapses. Let's take a look at a case of precisely that happening.

> *An executive team I worked with was struggling with some pretty dysfunctional dynamics. As with most teams, there were layers of history to the members' relationships, with all of them nursing feelings of being misjudged, maligned and/or exposed by their colleagues at some point. Individually, they would go to the CEO and criticise each other while trying to win support and favour for themselves.*

> *In executive meetings they avoided openly discussing the rifts in the team, each of them wearing a thin mask of politeness while being plainly passive-aggressive.*
>
> *The CEO was frustrated and keen to address the situation, but was unsure of how or where to start – and they also didn't see the part that they themselves were playing in keeping these unhelpful dynamics alive by not closing the unhelpful conversations down and facilitating the right discussions to take place. I suggested having one-to-one conversations with each team member to gain some understanding of their perspective, create clarity around new behavioural expectations, and outline the consequences for each of them if they didn't get on board.*
>
> *Overall, these conversations went well. Buoyed with confidence, the CEO then spoke with the team collectively to reiterate the expectations about intra-team conduct, emphasise the example that meeting these expectations would set for the rest of the organisation, and restate what the consequences would be for those who failed to meet them.*
>
> *Unfortunately, that's where it stopped. The team behaved well for a few weeks, but old habits die hard: it wasn't long before the former dynamics and behaviours were back to where they were before the 'line-in-the-sand' conversations. And the CEO as well gradually fell back into their old role of enabling this situation.*

As we learned in Chapter 2, accountability doesn't necessarily come easily or naturally to us – so whether we are the Accountee or the Accountor, if we can find a way to avoid it, all too often we will. In the situation described above, after having asked for an explanation of past behaviours, set up expectations of new ones, and made it clear that they would be evaluating how well the team members were abiding by these rules, the CEO became a toothless tiger by not following through as the bad behaviours crept back in.

Because the recurrences of these behaviours were not called out as they happened or addressed in conversations afterwards, the Consequences leg of the stool was missing, and so the whole thing fell over. And the same can happen with either of the other two legs: if the Explanation of accountability isn't provided or the party providing the Evaluation isn't 'salient' (e.g., does not have the appropriate level of authority or lacks the required expertise), you better believe that stool will still fall over – in fact, probably a whole lot earlier.

THE INNER WORKINGS OF ACCOUNTABILITY

Now that we've defined the three key components of accountability, let's dig beneath the surface to understand a bit more about its inner workings, and the implications they have for how we can move from *holding* to *calling* to account.

Accountability – it's all in your head

As we saw in the definition above, accountability is *perceived*. So while it has very real consequences, it operates in the perceptual domain, which means it is considered a 'state of mind' rather than a 'state of affairs'. It exists in your head rather than as a situation or set of circumstances – we spoke to this in Chapter 2 when we explored the 'Internal' psychological perspective of accountability.

This is HUGE – not only because it explains why there is such variance in how different individuals perceive their accountability, but also because it helps determine how they cope with the demands of it. It also explains why even the best accountability processes and systems will only get you so far, because there's very little chance that you, your peers, or your team members will interpret and understand them in the same way.

What this means is that we can't rely on accountability processes and systems to do the heavy lifting. As accountability is fundamentally subjective, we need to take a human-centred approach, one that values people and their perspectives and is committed to helping them feel well and do well.

Accountability – nurture or nature?

If accountability is a state of mind rather than a state of affairs, what does that mean in terms of its stability? You may have heard the term 'nature versus nurture', which speaks to whether something is fixed and an inherent aspect of an individual (their *nature*, also known as *trait-based*), or is changeable and influenced by the individual's environment (their *nurture*, also known as *state-based*).

Because it has been found to be dynamic, changeable and reliant on factors in the workplace environment such as leaders, team members and culture, individual accountability can be considered to be state-based (nurture) rather than *trait-based* (nature).

This makes sense. Accountability doesn't happen in a vacuum, so our perceptions of accountability are the result of both a range of contextual factors, well as the quality of relevant accountability relationships.

The fact that accountability is fundamentally state-based is good news: it means that it is open to influence, and as such, numerous aspects of the workplace environment (you, the team, the culture as a whole) can be intentionally managed to leverage it.

Accountability – an inside job?

Where does accountability come from? Well, in similar fashion to motivation, research suggests that sources of accountability can be *external*, *internal*, or a combination of both.

With *external accountability*, we feel obligated to perform certain behaviours because we are expected to do so by others. With *internal accountability*, we feel the obligation to perform certain behaviours because of our own commitment to it or the expectations we have of ourselves.

This distinction is useful to understand, as it has implications for explaining and predicting behaviour. When individuals perceive *internal accountability*, the required behaviours or outcomes are aligned with their own values, beliefs and self-concept, which creates a perceived *obligation to oneself*. They will voluntarily fulfil these accountability expectations and, just as intrinsically motivated people work hard in the absence of extrinsic rewards, people with high internal accountability will behave as though they are accountable regardless of the support they receive from accountability partners.

However, when individuals perceive *external accountability*, they are likely to perform behaviours mostly because of the perceived need to deliver outcomes to others. This can mean that the accountability has less personal meaning, is less aligned with their values and beliefs, and consequently they feel less obligation to fulfil it.

Because of these differences, internal sources of accountability require less managing and supervision than external sources. Formal control mechanisms – role descriptions, performance appraisals, rewards and punishments, and so on – may not be necessary, as the sources of accountability align with an individual's values, beliefs and self-concept. So getting to know both yourself and the people you are calling to account so that you can be intentional and explicit about this alignment is the smart thing to do.

FROM HOLDING TO CALLING

In order to support ourselves and the people we lead to do their best work, we need to understand and accept that people don't function like machines. Each of us is a living system that needs meaningful work and connections to consistently show up at their best. The shift from *holding* to *calling* resets the accountability dynamic to meet this need.

The three 'below-the-surface' insights about accountability that we explored above – the fact that it is *perceptual* and *subjective*; that it is *state-based* rather than trait-based; and that *internal accountability* is far more powerful than external accountability – help us understand what we need to do to instigate this shift.

Make no mistake, this is no small task: we are moving from *driving* action through fear, consequences and accountability systems, to *inspiring* it through a human-centred approach founded in love and possibility.

This shift triggers changes in our brain and body, as it moves us out of fight-or-flight and survival mode and towards confidence, connection and growth. As we begin to feel seen and known, our feelings of safety also increase, and our perspective changes from being 'me'-focused to looking outward, encompassing 'we' and 'us'. We move from operating 'below the line' – where the culture is one of domination and competition, of 'you' versus 'me' – to 'above the line', where we begin to understand the common experiences that connect us all, and a culture of partnering and collaboration begins to take shape.

Understanding the perfectly imperfect nature of each of us allows us to let go of the need to be 'on' all the time – the need to always be right, to look good and be perfect. We are able to bump up against the edges of our humanity, understand that learning comes through experience, and that only by showing up to do the work can we benefit, contribute and learn forward so that we can get it *more* right next time.

In this space, rather than pointing fingers at others and playing the victim, we own what is ours to own and become the authors of our actions, outcomes and destiny. Rather than avoiding the discomfort inherent in challenge, uncertainty and change, we move towards it with openness and a willingness to learn, understanding that we may not have all the answers and that feelings of struggle don't always mean that we are incapable or wrong.

In moving from *holding* to *calling*, the drama of naming, blaming and shaming exits stage left, the corrosive corridor conversations evaporate, and the stifling culture of fake politeness takes its leave. And in their place, positive, purposeful progress is given the space to emerge.

	HOLDING TO ACCOUNT	**CALLING TO ACCOUNT**
Driver	Fear	Confidence (love)
Focus	Survival	Growth
Perspective	Inward (me)	Outward (we/us)
Operating from…	Below the line	Above the line
Attitude	Competition (you vs. me)	Collaboration (us together)
Motivation	External (or none)	Internal
Mindset	Fixed (look good/stay safe)	Benefit (learn forward/contribute)
Locus of control	They/You	Me/I
Self-talk	Victim	Author
Energy	Avoid	Advance
Behaviour	Passive/actively avoidant	Actively advancing
Result	Underperformance	Actively advancing

Table 3.1: From holding to calling to account

The question is, how can we make this shift?

In the next two chapters, we explore the factors that my research found make the most difference in us moving from holding to calling people to account: the clarity of accountability expectations and the quality of accountability relationships.

SUMMARY

» When we hold people to account, accountability is used as a form of discipline that is based in power and fear.

» Fear-based accountability stifles the creativity and innovation that teams and organisations need to face challenges and make the most of opportunities.

» Research suggests that accountability comprises three elements, all of which must be present if it is to function properly:

1. **Explanation** to the Accountee of the parameters of their accountability,

2. **Evaluation** of the Accountee's fulfilment of their responsibilities by a relevant Accountor, and

3. **Consequences** as a result of this evaluation.

» There are three key internal dynamics of accountability, the understanding of which will help us move from holding to calling people to account:

- Accountability is perceived – it is fundamentally subjective, which means that we can't rely on accountability processes and systems to do the work for us.

- Accountability is state-based rather than trait-based – even as it is subjective, accountability is open to influence by factors in the workplace environment that can be mobilised to positively encourage it.

- Accountability is most effective when it is internal rather than external – when our understanding of our accountability aligns with our own values, beliefs and self-concept, we require less managing and support than when it is imposed upon us by an outside authority.

» The alternative to the fear-based holding people to account is calling them to account from a place of love, which allows our bodies and brains to dial down the survival instinct and move towards confidence, connection and growth, resulting in less fear, less drama, less conflict, and positive, purposeful progress.

FROM IDEAS TO ACTION

- As an Accountor, start taking notice of how often you *hold* people to account as opposed to *calling* them to account.

    » How does your mindset, language, energy and behaviour differ in each situation?

    » What impact does each approach have on yourself, on your Accountees, and on progress and performance overall?

- Now think about the situations and relationships in which your role is the Accountee. Evaluate how often you are *held* to account for your responsibilities rather than being *called* to account.

    » How does each approach make you feel?

    » What impact does each have on your motivation, engagement, performance and wellbeing?

References

'Leadership experts Ron Heifetz and Marty Linsky refer to these kinds of challenges as 'adaptive'...' Heifetz, R. & Linsky, M. (2002, June). A survival guide for leaders. *Harvard Business Review, 80*(6), 65-74.

'In the academic literature, accountability is defined as "a perceived expectation that one's decisions or actions will be evaluated by a salient audience"...' Hall, A. T. & Ferris, G. R. (2011). Accountability and extra-role behavior. *Employee Responsibilities and Rights Journal, 23*(2), 131-144.

'Accountability operates in the perceptual domain, which means it is considered a "state of mind" rather than a "state of affairs"...' Lerner, J. S. & Tetlock, P. E. (1999). Accounting for the effects of accountability. *Psychological Bulletin, 125*(2), 255.

'Individual accountability can be considered to be "state-based" rather than "trait-based"...' Hall, A. T. & Ferris, G. R. (2011). Accountability and extra-role behavior. *Employee Responsibilities and Rights Journal, 23*(2), 131-144.

'In a similar way to motivation, research suggests that sources of accountability can be internal or external...' Ebrahim, A. (2003). Accountability in practice: Mechanisms for NGOs. *World Development, 31*(5), 813-829.

'Just as intrinsically motivated people work hard in the absence of extrinsic rewards...' Amabile, T. M., Hill, K. G., Hennessey, B. A. & Tighe, E. M. (1994). The work preference inventory: Assessing intrinsic and extrinsic motivational orientations. *Journal of Personality and Social Psychology, 66*(5), 950.

4.

CREATING CLARITY OF ACCOUNTABILITY EXPECTATIONS

'What does it feel like to be micromanaged?'

I'VE ASKED THIS QUESTION MANY TIMES AS I'VE WORKED WITH executives, leaders and teams across business, government, NGOs and beyond. The answers typically sound something like these:

> 'Demotivating.'
> 'Undermines your confidence.'
> 'Frustrating.'
> 'Shows a lack of trust.'

I get it – I've been there. And I'm sure you have, too.

It's not surprising that research shows that being micromanaged negatively impacts performance, innovation, teamwork, and individual health and wellbeing. When we are micromanaged, it can feel like an insult: an insult to our experience, an insult to our expertise, and an insult to our integrity and ability to deliver what's needed from us.

So, why do we feel the need to micromanage?

CLOSING THE ACCOUNTABILITY GAP

Micromanaging comes from a need for control. It is based in fear and is driven by a desire to feel a greater degree of safety. It's also a common response that I see from leaders when they feel team members aren't stepping into accountability in the way they *believe* is needed. And so, to fill the gap and increase their feelings of safety, the leader begins to micromanage.

But there is another, more effective way to prevent an accountability gap, or to bridge it if you feel that one is emerging. And that is to be crystal clear about expectations.

Research suggests that *clarity of accountability expectations* is one of two critical factors that drive accountability success. And as I work with leaders and teams, I see the same. And that's because clarity precedes action. Once we are clear about and agreed on what needs to happen, we can get on with doing it more effectively.

As we covered in Part I, accountability is *subjective*, and is based on the *perceptions* of the Accountee rather than attributions of accountability of an Accountor(s). Issues arise when there is a gap between these two perspectives.

Sounds simple, right?

> *Clarity of accountability expectations is one way that we can close the accountability gap.*

Unfortunately, my experience tells me – as I'm sure yours does too – it's often not that straightforward. So to help you get a better sense of what's involved, we can break down the relationship between accountability and clarity of expectations into three components:

- the **Terms** of accountability
- the **Type** of accountability and
- the **Six Ws** of accountability.

Let's look at each in more detail.

The terms: 'Accountable' vs. 'responsible'

One of the most common problems that I see in the teams and organisations I work with is with the language of accountability, and specifically the way in which the words 'accountability' and 'responsibility' are used interchangeably. This feeds the *confusion* problem that we explored in Chapter 1.

The thing is, it doesn't have to. That's because these terms have distinct definitions that are valuable to understand so that we can use them appropriately.

In project management, accountability and responsibility are pragmatically differentiated through the RACI framework. This acronym stands for the four roles that various stakeholders might play in any project:

- **R**esponsible
- **A**ccountable
- **C**onsulted
- **I**nformed

The framework is used to create an RACI matrix – also known as a responsibility assignment chart – that maps out every task, milestone or key decision involved in completing a project and assigns which roles are **R**esponsible for each action item, which personnel are **A**ccountable, and, where appropriate, who needs to be **C**onsulted or **I**nformed.

I really like the practical nature of the definitions used for accountability and responsibility in RACI, as they are easily translated into the way work is done in groups, teams and organisations. They are as follows:

- **Accountable** – this is the person or stakeholder who is *the 'owner' of the work*, and who must provide their sign-off or approval when the task, objective or decision is complete. This person must make sure that responsibilities are assigned for all activities related to the work. There is *only one person who is accountable* – so basically, 'the buck stops here'.

- **Responsible** – these are the people or stakeholders who *do the work*. They are the ones who must complete the task or objective or make the necessary decisions. This means that, potentially, *several people can be jointly responsible* – 'the work is done here'.

I've seen the difference that creating clarity around this use of language can have in a team, and it is quite amazing.

Once these terms are clearly defined, the work then becomes about ensuring that, as accountability is 'cascaded' down through the organisation and/or the team(s), the corresponding responsibilities go with it. This makes the accountability-responsibility trail clear.

The critical thing to remember is that *delegation of responsibility must include a level of accountability as well*. Here's an example of what I mean:

> *A CFO client of mine was accountable ('buck stops here') for preparing the firm's annual report. As a senior leader, it wasn't necessary or appropriate that she do all the tasks required to complete the report, and so she delegated responsibility ('work is done here') for some sections of the report to members of her leadership team. In delegating responsibility, she also made clear their accountabilities – that is, what 'the buck stops here' looked like for each of them in relation to the sections of the report that they were responsible for completing.*

> *This clarity of accountability expectations gave the leadership team the confidence, autonomy and authority to further delegate responsibility to members of their teams to gather the information that would go into the sections of the annual report that they were drafting. At this point, they too defined what the 'the buck stops here' looked like for each of their team members by defining the specific information they needed to gather, the format it needed to be presented in, and the timeline required for the data to be ready so that the report section could be submitted to the CFO on time.*
>
> *By defining and using accountability and responsibility as different but complementary terms, the CFO was able to be clear about expectations and cascade the appropriate levels of each through her team. It also provided an accountability/responsibility 'trail' that meant everyone knew where the work was being done and by whom, which eliminated double handling of tasks and reduced underperformance.*

The easiest way I've found to keep track of the accountability/responsibility trail is to create a tree diagram that maps the cascade. You can see an example in Figure 4.1 that follows.

> **Remember:**
>
> *Clarity precedes action. Once accountability and responsibility are clearly defined and the trail is clear, progress accelerates.*

Types of accountability

The second factor to consider when it comes to clarity of expectations is the type(s) of accountability that you are asking for or is being asked of you. While it may sound simple, this is actually a very complex, multi-layered concept that can be broken down into four different factors:

- *Task behaviours* vs. *Contextual behaviours*
- *Specific accountability* vs. *General accountability*
- *Process accountability* vs. *Outcome accountability*
- *Formal accountability* vs. *Informal accountability*

Let's take a look at each of these areas in turn.

TASK BEHAVIOURS VS. CONTEXTUAL BEHAVIOURS

We commonly think of accountability in relation to task performance. These *task behaviours* usually transform raw materials into goods and services, and as such directly perform the core functions of a business or organisation – things like manufacturing goods, servicing customers, or developing new products. At an even more micro level, these are the specific task details in the description of what you are required to do in your role.

But there is another set of behaviours that supports the core function of the team or organisation by contributing to its social and psychological environment. These are called *contextual behaviours*, and can include such things as how often and how willing team members are to help each other, and how much they go above and beyond their position descriptions through extra-role behaviours to contribute to the team or organisation.

Both task behaviours and contextual behaviours are necessary for an organisation's wellbeing, and, therefore, are of value to teams and organisations. However, in my experience, issues with accountability related to clarity of expectations arise more often in relation to contextual behaviours than task behaviours.

An area in which I see this problem most often is when it comes to employees 'living the values of the organisation' – a concept that definitely falls under the category of contextual behaviours! Having clarity and consistency about what these values *are*, communicating this to

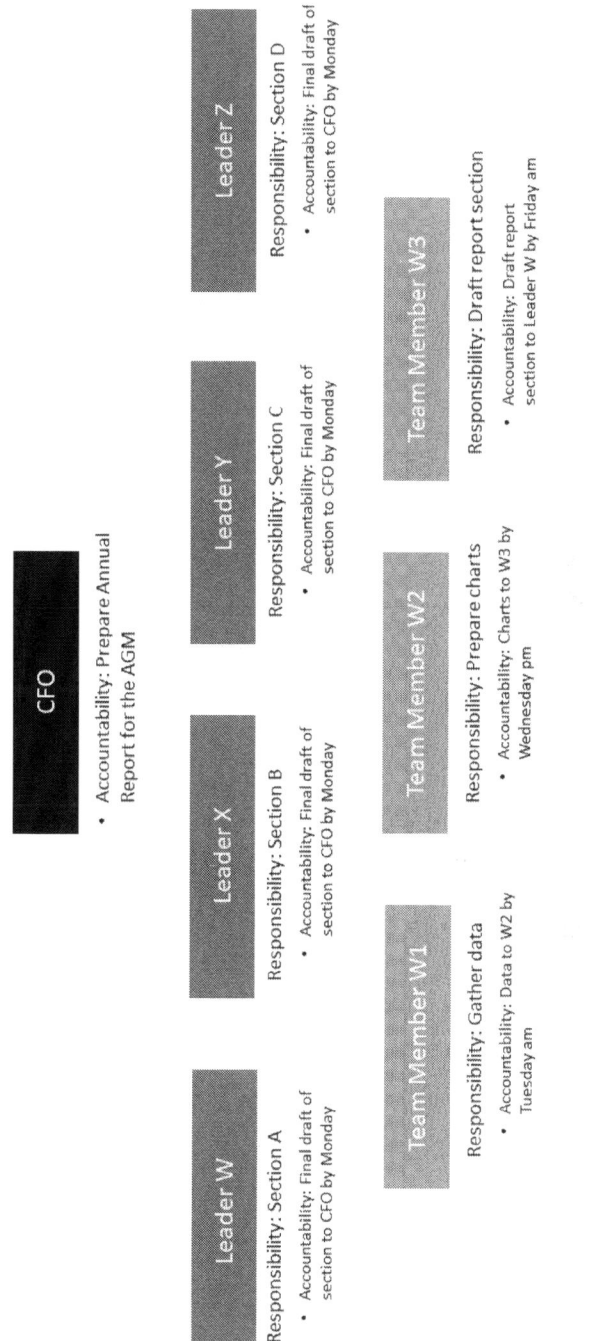

CREATING CLARITY OF ACCOUNTABILITY EXPECTATIONS

CFO
- Accountability: Prepare Annual Report for the AGM

Leader W
Responsibility: Section A
- Accountability: Final draft of section to CFO by Monday

Leader X
Responsibility: Section B
- Accountability: Final draft of section to CFO by Monday

Leader Y
Responsibility: Section C
- Accountability: Final draft of section to CFO by Monday

Leader Z
Responsibility: Section D
- Accountability: Final draft of section to CFO by Monday

Team Member W1
Responsibility: Gather data
- Accountability: Data to W2 by Tuesday am

Team Member W2
Responsibility: Prepare charts
- Accountability: Charts to W3 by Wednesday pm

Team Member W3
Responsibility: Draft report section
- Accountability: Draft report section to Leader W by Friday am

Figure 4.1: The RACI model in action

the organisation, and also communicating expectations for *how* team members embody them in the daily performance of their duties are critical steps that I often see missed. The message this gives is that task behaviours are more important than contextual ones.

The consequence? It makes managing 'lone wolves' far more difficult and complex than it needs to be. You know these people: they may be high performers in terms of task behaviours, but make no effort in the area of contextual behaviours, and as a result are a toxic influence on team culture. Over time, this double standard erodes both task and contextual behaviours across the team and contributes to underperformance.

Task and contextual behaviours comprise different aspects of performance in teams and organisations. We certainly *perceive* and *expect* accountability for these different types of behaviour, which means that it is valuable to understand and identify any accountability gaps that may exist with either one, or both.

> **The bottom line is:**
>
> *Whether you're asking for accountability (Accountor) or being asked for it (Accountee), you need to be clear about the expectations for both task and contextual behaviours.*

SPECIFIC ACCOUNTABILITY VS. GENERALISED ACCOUNTABILITY

When it comes to the objective of accountability, we can think of it as being either *specific* or *generalised*.

With *specific accountability*, we are likely to feel the need to perform specific behaviours, but may not feel the obligation to go beyond these. For example, we may attend team meetings, but make no contribution to them.

With *generalised accountability*, we feel the need to perform a broad range of behaviours that are not specific. Further, we are motivated to perform these behaviours regardless of whether they are explicitly requested of us or if we receive an immediate or equivalent return on our investment of our body's mental and physical 'resources' (energy, attention, action).

We can see from this, then, that generalised accountability taps into the ideas of *internal accountability* and intrinsic motivation that we discussed in Chapter 3. This makes sense, as generalised accountability objectives provide the Accountee with greater levels of autonomy in how they meet the expectations, which has been shown to increase productivity and positive affect/mood as well as job satisfaction.

PROCESS ACCOUNTABILITY VS. OUTCOME ACCOUNTABILITY

In addition to thinking of accountability through specific or generalised objectives, researchers have distinguished between a concept of accountability that evaluates the means, or how the tasks are done (which we refer to as *process accountability*), and one that evaluates the ends, or the outcomes of the tasks (known as *outcome accountability*). They have found that process and outcomes accountability have different effects on the way we think and make decisions.

Process accountability has been shown to lead to a higher level of cognitive engagement in decision-making tasks and, thereby, to higher-quality decisions in the completion of the accountability task(s). One explanation for this is that there is an expectation that the *way of working* will be evaluated as part of the overall accountability evaluation, and so more focus and attention is given to that as tasks are completed.

In contrast, a focus on outcome accountability appears to lead us to use less complex or inconsistent cognitive processes about how the work is done, and to engage in anticipatory self-justification ('it's okay to do it this way, the ends justifies the means') and impression management (denying or explaining away negative events or behaviours to avoid disapproval).

This aligns with Carol Dweck's work on growth and fixed mindset and the importance of setting goals that encourage development and learning, with the achievements occurring as a by-product. Doing so encourages people to be innovative and stretch their boundaries, rather than playing it safe to 'look good'. It also speaks to the research of Teresa Amabile and Stephen Karmer, which suggests that a clear sense of progress meeting a clear series of events or milestones is the most important influence on what makes employees feel enthusiastic about work. And, finally, it means that it's no longer possible for people to get away with achieving desired KPIs by behaving badly.

FORMAL ACCOUNTABILITY VS. INFORMAL ACCOUNTABILITY

Our final type distinction is that between *formal* and *informal accountability*, which first became a topic of interest with the famous Hawthorne studies of 1924-32, and has been continued in the work of such researchers as Gretchen Helmke and Steven Levitsky.

In this schema, *formal accountability* comes from expectations that are created, communicated and enforced through official channels, such as accountability processes and systems.

Informal accountability is found in socially shared expectations (usually unwritten) that are created, communicated and enforced outside official channels. This is most often seen in the subculture of teams – that is, 'the way we do things around here' at the local level. For example, there may be an expectation that everyone comes to a weekly team meeting with one struggle, one win, and one learning from their week. This requirement isn't written into anyone's role description, nor is it part of a formal accountability system, but because of our need to belong we will fall in line with social norms created by the group. This is the power of informal accountability.

As we think about giving and receiving accountability and stepping into specific responsibilities, it is useful to be aware of whether the accountability that is expected of us is formal or informal. If you're feeling overwhelmed and overburdened, try making a list of all of the accountability expectations and obligations you perceive are being asked of you and then go through and assess whether they are formal or informal.

In my experience, I've seen that informal accountability can lead us to 'carry other people's water' and take on responsibilities that are not ours to own. Taking a step back and assessing whether what is being asked of you is formally required or an unspoken social norm may be a good place to begin rebalancing your accountability load.

Okay, so have you got all of that?
I don't blame you if not!

Talking about the type of accountability that we are asking for or is being asked of us necessitates many tiers of definition. To recap, and help you keep the distinctions clear, you can refer to Table 4.1 that follows.

Understanding the different types of accountability and the impact they have on our own (and others') thoughts, motivation and behaviour helps us be more effective in establishing, managing and meeting expectations.

Whether you're an Accountor or an Accountee, it's useful to understand these different types of accountability and how they function so that you can be more effective in shifting the dynamic away from *holding* to account towards *calling* to account. The type(s) that are applicable will vary depending on your specific accountability situation, but knowing that these are the 'levers' that you can adjust, you can begin to create the optimal accountability context to make the positive, purposeful progress you are hoping for.

The Six Ws

We're now at the nitty-gritty end of the clarity conversation, where we need to be clear about the specifics of the accountability we're asking for (if we're the Accountor) or being asked to provide (if we're the Accountee).

To do this, we can employ a useful tool called the Six Ws, which is used in everything from journalism, academic research and police investigations to Six Sigma approaches to project management. I was first taught the Six Ws by my English teacher, but they originally came from a poem by the famous author Rudyard Kipling, which begins:

> *I keep six honest serving-men*
> *(They taught me all I knew);*
> *Their names are What and Why and When*
> *And How and Where and Who.*

That's right: we're talking about those six basic questions that we all learned in school. And when it comes to accountability, they provide a useful 'checklist' to help us ensure that expectations are looked at from a number of different perspectives.

Why do we need these? Well, as an Accountor, we can't give what we haven't got – if we're not clear on each of these, then it's unlikely our Accountee(s) will be, and that leads us down a direct route to underperformance.

Providing our Accountees with all the relevant information gives the clarity they need to fulfil the expectations we have of them. And asking the right questions of our Accountor provides the clarity we need to set the goalposts for accountability.

As an Accountee, the reality is that we may sometimes (perhaps even often) need to 'manage up' when it comes to accountability, and compel our Accountor to provide the information we require to have complete clarity of expectations. The bonus is that this provides

TYPE OF ACCOUNTABILITY	DEFINITION
Task behaviours	Those behaviours that directly perform the *core functions* of a business or organisation
Contextual behaviours	Those behaviours that contribute to the *social and psychological* environment of a business or organisation
Specific accountability	Explicit, externally imposed expectations that we feel obliged to meet, but not exceed
Generalised accountability	Implicitly understood or perceived expectations that we feel obliged to meet regardless of personal 'return on investment'
Process accountability	Evaluation based on the means – *how* we get the work done – which allows for greater autonomy, learning, creativity and innovation
Outcome accountability	Evaluation based on the ends – *what* was achieved – which encourages pre-set patterns, avoidance of innovation, and anticipatory self-justification
Formal accountability	Expectations created, communicated and enforced through official channels (e.g., accountability processes and systems)
Informal accountability	Expectations that derive from unwritten, socially shared expectations that are created, communicated and enforced outside official channels (e.g., team and group norms)

Table 4.1: Types of accountability

greater clarity for our Accountor as well, or, at a minimum, highlights those areas where they need to get more information or do more thinking about the expectations that we're being asked to deliver.

Let's have a look at each of the Six Ws in turn, and how asking them at the beginning can help us set accountability up for success.

WHY

Simon Sinek famously suggested we 'start with why' to connect to the energy of meaning and purpose, and attain a perspective that is larger than the 'here and now'. 'Why' questions help us understand and make sense of things in relation to each other and in context. Getting clear on this question will help generate motivation, as the Accountee will be able to articulate the benefits that the work is to deliver and how it fits into a 'bigger picture'.

Examples of Why questions could be:

- Why are we doing this work?
- Why does it matter to the team/business/organisation?
- Why do our clients/customers want/need it?
- Why this specifically (as opposed to other options)?
- Why is this a priority (in relation to other work that may be being asked for)?
- Why now?
- Why me/this team?

WHAT

This question is very simply about the requirements of the task and the scope of expectations. Understanding the different types of accountability (see above) can be useful here to ensure that nothing has been missed in the original briefing, and that clear boundaries are established so as to avoid accountability 'scope creep'.

Examples of What questions could be:

- What is the work to be done?
- What work has been done in this area/with this client before?

HOW

Including 'How' in our thinking around accountability not only provides an opportunity to consider the *task behaviours* needed to meet the expectations of the task, but also the *contextual behaviours* that the task will entail. Making clear what is and isn't acceptable behaviour at this point can save a lot of time and energy down the track if they are not being met.

Examples of How questions could be:

- How is the work expected to be done?
- How has it been done in the past?
- How else could it be done if this isn't possible?

WHO

'Who' questions create the 'human network map' for accountabilities: they help to identify reporting lines, liaison relationships, collaboration opportunities and challenges, sources of support, and relevant stakeholder groups. And, if things go wrong, understanding who needs to be informed and who can help is critical.

Examples of Who questions could be:

- Who are the stakeholders involved?

- Who is accountable ('the buck stops here')?
- Who is responsible ('the work is done here')?
- Who will lead?
- Who will support?
- Who will sponsor?
- Who will ultimately benefit?

WHEN

Time deadlines on key milestones, outputs and outcomes are an important part of accountability expectations, but of equal importance is the scheduling and frequency of accountability check-ins. Having expectations around this so that it is normalised as the work progresses helps to ensure a regular flow of information and connection, which generally minimises nasty surprises down the track.

Also, if the work requires collaboration across time zones or in a hybrid work environment, this adds another layer of complexity to the question of 'when' and needs to be considered.

Examples of When questions could be:

- When is the work expected to be completed by?
- When are the critical time milestones?
- When should I be checking in with you to measure progress?

WHERE

With the increase in dispersed teams and flexible work practices, the formerly simple question of where the work is to be done is not necessarily so simple any more. Answering it may require that new ways of coordination and collaboration be considered.

CREATING CLARITY OF ACCOUNTABILITY EXPECTATIONS

Examples of Where questions could be:

- Where is the work expected to be done?
- Where else could it be done if this isn't possible?
- Where has it been done in the past?

Using the Six Ws framework supports us to be clear and comprehensive about expectations so that there are no surprises in the accountability journey.

As we established at the very beginning of this book, confusion about accountability is the foundational issue in the epidemic of underperformance that is plaguing teams and organisations. With our increasingly complex workplace structures and dynamics, matters of accountability are often unclear at best and unintelligible at worst. This is compounded by the perceptual and subjective nature of accountability, which means that there can be multiple interpretations of the same accountability situation.

If you're the person asking for accountability (the Accountor), you need to be clear in your own mind on the Why, What, How, Who, When and Where of the work you're asking for so that you can have effective set-up, progress and follow-up conversations. And if you're the person being asked for accountability (the Accountee), you need to be clear on these Six Ws too, so that you know what is being asked and expected of you and can raise any questions, queries or concerns about delivering them.

'CLEAR IS KIND'

In her book *Daring Greatly: How the Courage to Be Vulnerable Transforms the Way We Live, Love, Parent, and Lead*, Brené Brown suggests that 'Clear is kind, unclear is unkind.' While she was referring to feedback conversations, I think the exact same thing applies to expectations around accountability.

When accountability expectations are confused, this is typically because one or more of the Six Ws is unclear. This will have a different impact depending on which of these fundamental questions is unclear, but the overall effect is the same: more stress, drama and waste, and less progress, engagement and performance.

The level of clarity that comes from answering the Six Ws provides a sense of safety and control that means people feel confident in what they are being asked to deliver.

When accountability expectations are clear, people understand why they are doing the work, what needs to be done, and how it fits into a 'bigger picture'. They know who is involved, the critical timelines and milestones, and what the consequences are if they aren't met – for both themselves and the wider context. They also know what the progress markers are and how these will be reported and reviewed.

What this requires from us is a shift in mindset in which we own our role in setting up clear expectations as an Accountor, or asking for them as an Accountee. We don't assume knowledge or understanding and are clear about the responsibilities and accountabilities involved in the expectations that are being set. And we take the time and make a commitment to have the conversations needed to do this in a way that *calls* rather than *holds* people to account.

As I mentioned at the beginning of this chapter, clarity of expectations is the first part of using accountability to set us up for success. In the next chapter, we'll explore the second: the quality of accountability relationships.

SUMMARY

» *Clarity of expectations is the first of two critical factors that drive accountability success – once we are clear and agreed on what needs to happen, we can do it more effectively.*

» *Three areas can help increase the clarity of expectations:*

1. *The **Terms** of accountability – distinguishing between who is accountable (the 'owner' of the work) and who is responsible (those who will do the work) creates an 'accountability trail' that can be followed down through the organisation and within teams.*

2. *The **Type** of accountability – determining whether the accountability being asked of us relates to:*

   - *Task behaviours vs. Contextual behaviours*
   - *Specific accountability vs. Generalised accountability*
   - *Process accountability vs. Outcome accountability*
   - *Formal accountability vs. Informal accountability*

3. *The **Six Ws** – asking and answering these fundamental questions (Why, What, How, Who, When, Where) sets up both the Accountor and the Accountee for accountability success.*

» *Creating clarity of expectations requires a shift in mindset in which we maintain integrity in communication and commit to having the conversations that will allow us to call rather than hold people to account.*

FROM IDEAS TO ACTION

- Think about a current accountability challenge you have in your team. Map out the Six Ws for that challenge, taking into consideration the types of accountability that apply.
    - » Have you communicated these expectations clearly to the Accountee(s)?

- Have a check-in conversation with the Accountee(s) about their understanding of each of these expectations.
    - » What are the differences in your understanding of expectations versus theirs? Make a note of and align any differences so that you can move forward with clarity and confidence.

References

'**Being micromanaged negatively impacts performance, innovation, teamwork and individual health and wellbeing...**' White, R.D. (2010). The micromanagement disease: Symptoms, diagnosis, and cure. *Public Personnel Management, 39*(1), 71-76. https://doi.org/10.1177/009102601003900105

'**Research suggests that clarity of expectations is one of two critical factors that drive accountability success...**' Han, Y. & Perry, J. L. (2020). Conceptual bases of employee accountability: A psychological approach. *Perspectives on Public Management and Governance, 3*(4), 288-304.

'**Both task and contextual behaviours are necessary for an organisation's wellbeing and, therefore, are of value to teams and organisations...**' Motowidlo, S. J. & Van Scotter, J. R. (1994). Evidence that task performance should be distinguished from contextual performance. *Journal of Applied Psychology, 79*(4), 475; Mero, N. P., Guidice, R. M. & Werner, S. (2014). A field study of the antecedents and performance consequences of perceived accountability. *Journal of Management, 40*(6), 1627-1652.

'**Generalised accountability objectives provide the Accountee with greater levels of autonomy in how they meet the expectations...**' Johannsen, R. & Zak, P. J. (2020). Autonomy raises productivity: An experiment measuring neurophysiology. *Frontiers in Psychology, 11*, 963.

'**...which has been shown to increase productivity and positive affect/mood as well as job satisfaction...**' Wheatley, D. (2017). Autonomy in paid work and employee subjective wellbeing. *Work and Occupations, 44*(3), 296-328. https://doi.org/10.1177/0730888417697232

'**In addition to thinking of accountability through specific or generalized objectives, researchers...**' Siegel-Jacobs, K. & Yates, J. F. (1996). Effects of procedural and outcome accountability on judgment quality. *Organizational Behavior and Human Decision Processes, 65*(1), 1-17.

'**Process accountability has been shown to lead to a higher level of greater cognitive engagement in decision-making tasks and, thereby, to higher quality decisions**...' Markman, K. D. & Tetlock, P. E. (2000). Accountability and close-call counterfactuals: The loser who nearly won and the winner who nearly lost. *Personality and Social Psychology Bulletin, 26*(10), 1213-1224.

'**A focus on outcome accountability appears to lead us to use less complex or inconsistent cognitive processes and to engage in anticipatory self-justification and impression management**...' Morris, M. W. & Moore, P. C. (2000). The lessons we (don't) learn: Counterfactual thinking and organizational accountability after a close call. *Administrative Science Quarterly, 45*(4), 737-765.

'**This aligns with Carol Dweck's work on growth and fixed mindset**...' Dweck, C. (2006). *Mindset: The New Psychology of Success.* Random House.

'**Drawing on the work exploring formal and informal institutions**...' Helmke, G. & Levitsky, S. (2014). *Informal Institutions and Comparative Politics: A Research Agenda.* https://wcfia.harvard.edu/files/wcfia/files/883_informal-institutions.pdf

'**In her book** Daring Greatly...' Brown, B. (2012). *Daring Greatly: How the Courage to Be Vulnerable Transforms the Way We Live, Love, Parent, and Lead.* Avery.

5.

CULTIVATING QUALITY OF ACCOUNTABILITY RELATIONSHIPS

HAVE YOU EVER NOTICED HOW MUCH EASIER IT IS TO WORK WITH people you like? Communication is clearer and smoother; the work seems to take less effort and gets done more quickly; and, when things don't go to plan (which will inevitably happen at some point), it's easier to talk about it, which means issues get resolved more swiftly and with less drama.

And don't you find that it's a lot more enjoyable too? This is important, because our brains function differently when we're in a positive emotional state – in ways that help us be creative, solve problems, and make connections that we might not otherwise see.

These kinds of relationships are abundant in what's called *relational energy*. Research suggests that people who generate positive relational

energy – positive energisers – are higher performers and are four times more likely to succeed than people who have power or knowledge.

Just think about that for a moment:

Positive relational energy trumps formal power or knowledge by 400% in terms of outcomes and performance.

How is this possible?

It's because of something called the heliotropic effect, whereby all living systems tend to move towards positive energy and away from negative energy. Just as plants grow towards the sun, we also flourish in the presence of positive energy. Studies have found that this kind of energy impacts us at the cellular level, which is why more areas of our brains are activated when we experience positive emotions.

Once you understand this, it's probably not surprising that the *quality of accountability relationships* is the second of the two key factors that impact accountability.

FROM BARREN TO FRUITFUL ACCOUNTABILITY RELATIONSHIPS

As we've discussed already, lack of accountability keeps us fragile. It impacts everything we do, whether that's eating more healthily, being more active, meeting career or project milestones, or preparing for our weekly team meeting. Without it, what we say we're going to do becomes little more than wishful thinking. And that's a real issue, because social groups – including your team and your organisation – depend on accountability to function effectively.

So how does the quality of relationships impact accountability?

One of the most vital themes that emerged from the review of accountability research I conducted before writing this book was that the relationship between Accountor and Accountee has a direct and significant impact on accountability. Not just one or two aspects of it – *every* aspect, from systems and processes to communication and collaboration, team culture and dynamics to progress, performance and outcomes. This is why:

**For accountability relationships to be effective,
they need to be secure.**

'Secure' means they need to have as little fear involved as possible (preferably none), because when relationships are based in fear, they lack trust and safety. As a result:

- We avoid contact and interaction in a bid to stay safe.
- We 'muddle through' with the lack of clarity around our accountabilities and responsibilities, second-guessing and filling the gaps ourselves.
- We struggle on with too much to do and too little time and resources.
- We hide missteps and mistakes due to a fear of being ridiculed, shamed or 'demoted'.
- We defend underperformance to ourselves and others, preferring to see it as a result of 'the system', which is actually just code for the dysfunctional accountability dynamics in play.

The result is drama, stress, and a lack of learning and progress that creates and perpetuates underperformance. These are what I call *barren accountability relationships*. Why 'barren'? Because they are lifeless – they lack the nutrients to produce growth.

By contrast, *fruitful accountability relationships* are fuelled by positive relational energy between Accountor and Accountee. In these relationships, we feel secure in our connections because:

- We have high levels of trust and safety.
- We feel able to ask for help and support when needed.
- We communicate clearly, regularly and honestly about our performance – even when there are problems involved.

The result is learning and development. Confidence, capability and capacity grow, and progress and performance follow easily.

Importantly, you don't have to be 'best buddies' with someone to have a fruitful accountability relationship. High levels of positive relational energy come from behaviours such as showing concern for others, being flexible in thinking, valuing others, and even something as simple as smiling. Even more importantly, evidence suggests that these are all attributes that can be developed.

GETTING TO 'YES': THE FIVE SAFETY QUESTIONS

In my experience of both asking for accountability (as Accountor) and being asked for accountability (as Accountee), I've found that the question of whether I am in a fruitful accountability relationship or not comes down to the answers to these five questions:

1. Do I feel safe to stuff up, slip up and learn?
2. Do I feel safe to succeed and grow?
3. Do I feel safe to share my weaknesses?
4. Do I feel safe to shine in my strengths?
5. Do I feel safe to show up as 'authentically me'?

In Chapter 2, we looked at the neuroscience of accountability – how our brains respond to accountability situations by interpreting the incoming mental and physical data and devising a course of action. These five questions speak to the specific perceived 'threats' that can cause our brains to trigger an avoidance response that undermines accountability.

If we don't feel safe to acknowledge when we've *stuffed up or slipped up*, we'll try to cover those mistakes up and/or shift the blame afterwards rather than admitting them early and getting shared input on how best to move forward.

If we perceive that we are engaged in a competitive culture of 'you' versus 'me' with our peers, colleagues and boss, this means we feel that none of them are supportive of us *succeeding and growing*. Our perspective is is 'me-focused' rather than outward-looking: task accountability (getting the job done) takes priority over contextual accountability (how the work is done). This 'lone-wolf' culture makes accountability fragile as we get sucked into the need to show up perfectly all the time and not show any signs of weakness or failure.

If we feel it's not okay to *acknowledge weaknesses* and ask for support, we will just continue to muddle through, doing the best we can with what we've got. But in all likelihood, we'll be hating it, because let's face it – who enjoys doing things they know they're not good at? This is not good for our confidence, motivation, or the outcomes of the accountability expectations we are trying to meet.

If we don't feel safe to shine in our *strengths*, we may hold back and play small to make others feel like they're not being upstaged and protect our sense of connection and belonging. Unfortunately, this doesn't serve us, our accountabilities or our responsibilities, because we've let talent, possibility, and the opportunity to progress and perform lie fallow.

If we don't feel safe to show up as *authentically who we are* – be that in regard to race, gender, cultural background, or personal values and beliefs – then our brains will constantly be operating in a state of 'threat alertness'. Research tells us that we are less able to process information, solve problems and make connections (between data points and between each other) when our brains are in this heightened state – so how could this possibly be helpful for us in meeting our accountability expectations?

Fruitful accountability relationships don't always 'just happen'. They need tending, just like a tree sapling does: they need warmth, light, nourishment and fertiliser (but no bull-shit!). Depending on the health of the soil, the root system, and the tree itself, it may take time to bear fruit – to build the trust that will move this relationship towards a new basis. But make no mistake; until you can say a consistent 'yes' to these questions, the quality of your accountability relationship is limiting the degree to which accountability expectations will be met.

If you are the Accountor, your work here is in creating a context in which the 'yes' can be said willingly and wholeheartedly. This is about creating a context of love, where your Accountee trusts your invitation to help them play a bigger game.

If you are the Accountee, your task lies in developing the courage and the conviction to say 'yes', even when it feels like a stretch. This is about you trusting and owning your strengths, abilities, and capacity to ask for help and support when needed. It's about you choosing to play a bigger game – even if an explicit invitation isn't forthcoming.

SAFETY = SHOWING UP!

So the question is: how can we increase the safety in our accountability relationships – whether as Accountee or Accountor?

Answer: by *showing up* with a different picture of what 'good' looks like.

Research I've been involved with suggests (and other studies concur) that those leaders who are consistently delivering more positive outcomes for their teams and organisations see the world differently.

These leaders see that sustainable value isn't driven by their team's outcomes, but from the learning and growth that is reaped from their successes and their failures. This viewpoint allows them to create cultures in which people feel safe to learn.

The safety to fail, succeed, shine, and be vulnerable and authentic to oneself determine the quality of the accountability relationship and what is possible from it.

In our accountability relationships, feeling safe to learn helps us feel safe to NOT succeed, because we understand that failure is a part of learning and growth.

In a world filled with uncertainty and unpredictability, these leaders see that trying to completely control people and situations is a fool's errand. And this gives them the confidence to foster the capacity and possibility in others to continue generating new possibilities.

In our accountability relationships, fostering our capacity helps us feel safe to try new things and grow our confidence and capability without fear of being 'cut down'.

These leaders see that their people rarely function like orderly machines, but instead ebb and flow depending on what is happening within them and around them. They accept that we all have weaknesses, and that leading people is a messy and magical process that demands humility and curiosity.

In our accountability relationships, acceptance of our inherent weaknesses helps us to feel safe to struggle, to be 'not okay', and to ask for help and support when needed.

These leaders have let go of the need to be the expert who has all the answers their team needs, as this limits what they are able to achieve. Refusing this role provides them with the courage to invite people with diverse strengths, experiences and ideas – even some they don't agree with – to work as part of their teams.

In our accountability relationships, understanding that we each have a unique contribution to make and that by bringing our strengths together we will make progress and achieve the best performance helps us feel safe to shine in our strengths.

These leaders see that settling for compliance is a short-term strategy with limited benefits. They do the work to earn their people's long-term commitment by investing in meaningful coaching conversations and supporting self-organisation.

In our accountability relationships, being seen and known helps us feel safe to be authentic and bring our whole self to the relationship.

Fruitful accountability relationships make everything easier, from the most joyous successes to the hardest challenges and toughest problems. They are nurtured in the soil of mutual respect and trust, in understanding and accepting the unique, perfectly imperfect nature of each of us, and in the innate strengths, capacity and capability in us all.

Fruitful accountability relationships grow through consistently feeling safe and secure to show up and shine or slip up and stuff up. Relationships such as these leave behind the ego-driven nature of 'lone-wolf' cultures, understanding that we will always achieve more, better and faster if we work together. The result? Less drama, less stress, and less underperformance.

SUMMARY

- *Positive relational energy trumps formal power or knowledge by 400% in terms of outcomes and performance – this is why the quality of accountability relationships is the second critical factor for accountability success.*

- *Barren accountability relationships are fuelled by fear – as a result, we feel unsafe and go into 'survival mode', which leads to underperformance.*

- *Fruitful accountability relationships are fuelled by positive relational energy – as we feel secure in these connections, they support our learning and growth, and our confidence, capability and capacity to progress and perform follow in due course.*

- *Fruitful accountability relationships are present when we can consistently say 'yes' to the Five Safety Questions:*
    1. *Do I feel safe to stuff up/slip up and learn?*
    2. *Do I feel safe to succeed and grow?*
    3. *Do I feel safe to share my weaknesses?*
    4. *Do I feel safe to shine in my strengths?*
    5. *Do I feel safe to show up as 'authentically me'?*

- *As Accountors, we can nurture fruitful accountability relationships by creating a context of love, in which the 'yes' is said willingly and wholeheartedly because your Accountee trusts your invitation to help them play a bigger game.*

- *As Accountees, we can nurture fruitful accountability relationships by developing the courage and conviction to say 'yes' to the five questions and by actively choosing to play a bigger game.*

FROM IDEAS TO ACTION

- Think about the best accountability relationships that you've experienced – some in which you were the Accountor, and others in which you were the Accountee.
    - » What was the nature and quality of those relationships?
    - » For each of them, how would you have responded to the Five Safety Questions for each of them?
    - » What were the questions you felt most 'safe' saying yes to? Were there others that you felt less 'safe' saying yes to?
    - » If so, what impact did that have on the relationship?
- Now think about three current accountability relationships (in which you are either the Accountor or Accountee):

    A) one that you feel is going really well,
    B) one that you feel is going okay, and
    C) one that you feel is not going well.

For each of these accountability relationships, use the sliding scales below to rate how safe you feel for each of the Five Safety Questions, where 1 = not at all and 5 = 100% of the time.

Mark A, B, and C next to the number that corresponds to your answer for each relationship.

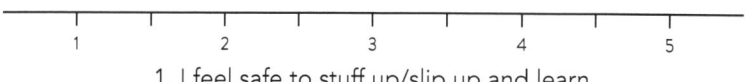

```
|----|----|----|----|----|----|----|----|
 1         2         3         4         5
```
1. I feel safe to stuff up/slip up and learn

|—————|—————|—————|—————|
1   2   3   4   5

2. I feel safe to succeed and grow

|—————|—————|—————|—————|
1   2   3   4   5

3. I feel safe to share my weaknesses

|—————|—————|—————|—————|
1   2   3   4   5

4. I feel safe to shine in my strengths

|—————|—————|—————|—————|
1   2   3   4   5

5. I feel safe to show up as 'authentically me'

What insights does this give you about how the relationships could be more fruitful? Make some notes in the spaces below.

Accountability Relationship A:
_____
_____
_____
_____

Accountability Relationship B:
_____
_____
_____
_____

Accountability Relationship C:
_____
_____
_____
_____

References

'Our brains function differently when we're in a positive emotional state...' Platt, M. (2020). *The Leader's Brain: Enhance Your Leadership, Build Stronger Teams, Make Better Decisions, and Inspire Greater Innovation with Neuroscience.* Wharton School Press.

'Research suggests that people who generate positive relational energy...' Baker, W. (2016, September). The more you energize your coworkers, the better everyone performs. *Harvard Business Review.* https://hbr.org/2016/09/the-energy-you-giv-off-at-work-matters

'This is because of something called the heliotropic effect...' Sheehan, A. (2014, July). *Finding the light in darkness: The heliotropic effect.* Center for Positive Organizations. https://positiveorgs.bus.umich.edu/news/finding-the-light-in-darkness-the-heliotropic-effect/

'Even more importantly, research shows that they are all attributes that can be developed...' Cameron, K. (2021). *Positively Energizing Leadership: Virtuous Actions and Relationships That Create High Performance.* Berrett-Koehler Publishers.

'Research I've been involved with suggests...' Leaders Lab 2021 Workplace Report.

'Research tells us that we are less able to process information, solve problems and make connections...' Fredrickson, B. L. (2013). Positive emotions broaden and build. In E. Ashby Plane & P. G. Devine (Eds.), *Advances in Experimental Social Psychology, 47,* 1-53. Academic Press.

PART II WRAP-UP

THE ACCOUNTABILITY RESET MATRIX

In order to address the epidemic of underperformance that's plaguing teams and organisations, we need to reset accountability and move from *holding* people to *calling* people to account. The two factors that will help us do this are the *clarity of accountability expectations* and the *quality of the accountability relationships* that we create. Understanding how these two factors interact can help us diagnose the cause of accountability issues that we may be facing and understand how we might begin to address them.

Let's use what I call the 'Accountability Reset Matrix' to understand how these drivers of accountability interact and create different scenarios that impact performance.

In Figure 5.1 that follows, the vertical axis shows the quality of accountability relationships, ranging from Barren to Fruitful. The horizontal axis denotes the clarity of accountability expectations, from Confused to Clear.

Confused Expectations + Barren Relationship = ACCOUNTABILITY EMERGENCY

When accountability expectations are confused and the accountability relationship is barren, there is little possibility that Accountees will reach out for the help or support that could improve the situation through asking for information about what is required of them and how they might achieve it. The lack of safety in the relationship means that the Accountee is 'me-focused,' and intent on staying safe and playing small.

This is a black hole for accountability, and a pit for progress and performance.

Confused Expectations + Fruitful Relationship = ACCOUNTABILITY ER

Even if the accountability relationship is fruitful, confused expectations can still result in underperformance. The good news is that, since the relationship is productive, clarity can improve with the right conversations.

So while progress is being limited here, much like a patient in the ER, the situation can be saved given the right treatment. If the confusion continues, though, it risks causing frustration that negatively impacts the quality of the relationship, which can then lead to an Accountability Emergency.

Clear Expectations + Barren Relationship = ACCOUNTABILITY COUNSELLING

When accountability expectations are clear but the relationship is barren, there is a fragility to the situation that may be tested when problems

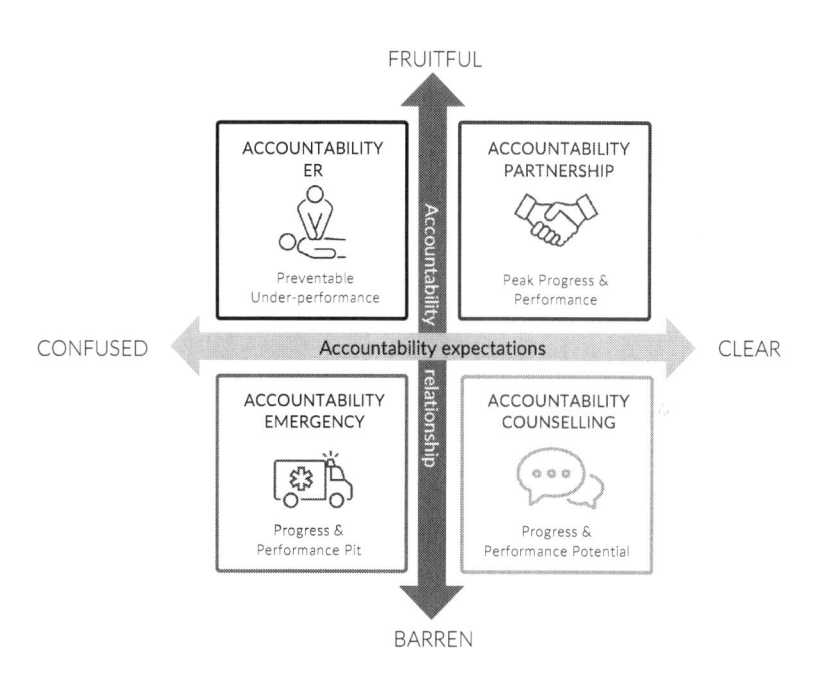

Figure 5.1: The Accountability Reset Matrix

arise. As we know, life rarely goes according to plan, and it is at these times that the quality of the accountability relationship makes a difference. The trust and psychological safety that are present in fruitful relationships support honest conversations about potential challenges and issues before they develop and enable collective problem-solving to resolve them.

So, there is performance and progress potential here if the relationship can be nurtured and developed.

Clear Expectations + Fruitful Relationship = ACCOUNTABILITY PARTNERSHIP

When accountability relationships are fruitful and expectations are clear, a true Accountability Partnership exists. In this situation people can question expectations, ask for support to fulfil them if needed, and feel confident in flagging issues as they arise along the way.

Reviews and progress check-ins are agreed upon, regular and transparent, and people take personal ownership for their accountability expectations. The focus is outwards, with a mindset of contribution and an understanding that 'What I do matters to the progress that we make together.'

This is where peak progress and performance lives.

The Accountability Reset Matrix can help us become clearer on the cause of our current accountability challenges and help identify the actions we can take to support peak performance and progress. Our goal is always to move our current challenge towards a true Accountability Partnership by starting to have the Accountability Reset conversations that need to happen.

It's also important to remember that yours is only one perspective of this accountability challenge. A powerful way I've found to begin Accountability Reset conversations is to ask the other person where they would place the current situation on the matrix. Understanding your different perspectives is a great way to open up conversations about how to get things on track.

After all, as leadership writer and researcher Margaret Wheatley so wisely says:

'Change starts with a conversation.'

FROM IDEAS TO ACTION

- Consider your most pressing accountability challenge right now, as either an Accountor or Accountee. Ask yourself the following questions:

    » Where would you place this situation on the matrix in terms of quality of accountability relationship and clarity of accountability expectations (Emergency, ER or Counselling)?

    » Which of the two key factors would help move this situation towards an Accountability Partnership – clarity of accountability expectations, or the quality of the accountability relationship?

    » What is the conversation that would support this positive shift? Who is it with? What questions would you need to ask?

PART III

HOW WE CAN BE BETTER AT IT

Bournemouth, England, May 2000.
I am general manager of a public aquarium on the south coast of England. Reporting to a board of directors, I've been brought in to shift the culture and lift performance of a team of around twenty-five staff ranging in age from sixteen to over sixty.

One of the most experienced and longest standing members of the team is our retail manager, who is also the person struggling the most with the changes I'm making.

In line with most retail operations, staff costs for our shop and catering areas are the highest variable cost. Tight margins mean they need to be managed closely, which requires the retail manager to be hands-on during shoulder periods and send staff home if visitor numbers are low.

We've met a number of times to discuss this. I've been clear about what needs to happen, and offered to look over the staff rota so we can decide together how to best meet the commercial needs.

It's now been three months, and while there have been some improvements, this month's trading figures show that they are not enough.

An added challenge is that the retail manager and one of the directors – my direct report – have a longer than twenty-year working relationship in the industry. The board is putting pressure on me to get the figures moving in the right direction more quickly, but when I spoke with my direct report about the possibility of moving the retail manager to performance management, he was not supportive.

It feels like I'm in a sandwich press. I'm being asked to deliver on what I've been brought in to do by the board, I'm not getting what I'm asking for from the retail manager, and my director isn't supporting the action I'd like to take to get things moving.

It's exhausting and demoralising.

WHEN ACCOUNTABILITY GOES WRONG, IT'S RARELY THE FAULT OF one thing or one person. This is not only because of the dynamic, perceptual nature of accountability that we explored in Chapter 2, but also because there are often multiple people and moving parts involved in any accountability scenario. And it's for these reasons that it's more accurate and useful to think of accountability as a system rather than a linear process.

In the most general sense, systems are simply a set of things working together as parts of an interconnecting network – a complex whole. A system can also be understood as a set of principles or processes by which something is done – an organised method.

The Accountability System that I detail in the chapters that follow is true to both of these meanings, in that it identifies the interconnecting moving parts of a more complex whole and also outlines a process through which these parts can be coordinated and organised. Further, it provides a structure that allows us to see how what we've covered so far fits together, and previews what's coming next.

These three interconnected moving parts of the Accountability System as shown in figure 7.1 are the Accountor(s), the Accountee(s), the Accountability Task(s), and the Accountability Context. We looked closely at the need for clarity of accountability expectations in defining accountability tasks in Chapter 4. Whether we are in the role of Accountor or Accountee, the first thing we need to make sure of is that we have our own personal accountability in place and are owning what's ours to own. We explore what this looks like in Chapter 6 when we discuss the Own It! mindset.

The dynamic interactions between the moving parts of the Accountor(s), the Accountee(s), and the task(s) are what bring the Accountability System to life and create the outcomes we want to achieve. In Chapter 7, we take a look at the first of these interactions: the *Accountability Set-up* – the time at which the Accountee and Accountor both perceive, understand and negotiate the accountability expectations of the task to be performed.

In Chapter 8, we examine the other two parts of the Accountability System: *the Accountability Exchange,* which is the nature of the interaction between Accountor and Accountee (as determined by the quality of the accountability relationship, which we covered in Chapter 5); and the *Accountability Response*, which is the specific situation in which the Accountee is called to account by the Accountor as they track progress along the way.

Finally, all of these elements and dynamics sit within the broader environment of the *Accountability Context.* In Chapter 9, we address this as we discuss how a culture of accountability can be intentionally crafted in our workplaces.

Our goal in understanding and leveraging the elements and interactions of the Accountability System is to create the Accountability Partnerships we defined at the end of Part II. Because the reality is that we need partners in accountability across all levels and teams in our organisations to remove the fragility and underperformance that's holding us back.

Figure 7.1: The Accountability System

6.

DO YOU OWN IT? DEVELOPING THE RIGHT MINDSET

HAVE YOU EVER PLAYED WORK PING-PONG?

Here's how the game typically goes:

There is work that both you and I have agreed to get done, and the deadline is looming.

You email me outlining how we could divide the responsibilities, and ask me to confirm if what you've proposed is okay, or to suggest ideas for how it could be done differently (PING).

I email back a list of problems and reasons why what you have proposed is not possible (PONG).

You ask if we can meet to discuss (PING).

I reply that I don't have time until two weeks next Tuesday (PONG).

You ask if we can arrange a ten-minute chat just to agree on first priorities for the next two weeks until we can meet (PING).

I send back a long email telling you how many other things I have to do right now, how other people are not pulling their weight, and that I don't have the mental space or energy to even talk about this right now (PONG).

You think, 'It probably took you longer than ten minutes to write that email,' agree to meet in two weeks, and start to get on with your to-dos on the list (PLONK).

Does the 'I' here sound like someone you know?

Could it even be you?

Work ping-pong is what we get pulled into when people avoid owning what's theirs to own. There is always a problem to be solved, and it's never up to them to solve it. These people suck us dry of time, energy and attention – our most precious resources – and create work for us that doesn't contribute to positive, purposeful progress. And also, let's face it – they are exhausting to deal with!

So why are some people like this?

Well it all comes down to mindset.

> **'Accountability is not just a question of nature or nurture. Accountability is a mindset that can be developed.'**
> **– CY WAKEMAN**

MINDSETS – WHY WE DO WHAT WE DO

Mindsets help us make sense of the world by simplifying and organising the information we need to process in any given moment. In every area of life, from work to home and everything in between, we are operating from a certain mindset that impacts what we see, think, feel and do.

Though mindsets were originally believed to be a purely psychological construct, it has now been confirmed that they have a physiological basis in our brains. Neuroscientists have identified mindsets as long-range neural connections that connect and integrate the three major regions of our brain:

   a. the *basal ganglia*, which are involved in the integration and selection of voluntary behaviour;

   b. the *limbic system*, which drives our behavioural and emotional responses (especially those connected with survival, such as feeding, reproduction and caring for our young, and fight-or-flight responses); and

   c. the *neocortex*, which commands higher functions such as sensory perception, emotion and cognition.

What this means is that mindsets effectively act as our brain's internal operating system, in that they:

- Filter the information from our environment that is most important,

- Interpret that filtered information in unique ways, and

- Activate and allocate various resources and traits (e.g., personality, skills, self-regulatory strategies) based upon that interpretation so that we can make decisions about how to best navigate the situations we encounter.

Our mindsets dictate what we see and how we interpret the world, which in turn shapes how we think, feel, show up and behave. They are why we do what we do.

This is why, in accountability situations, two different people can see or hear the same thing, yet interpret it differently and react to it differently. For instance, when presented with constructive criticism, one person might interpret it as, 'This is a threat,' and become defensive, whereas another could interpret it as, 'This is helpful,' and use it as an aid to learn and grow.

THE OWN IT! MINDSET

People with an Own It! mindset have what psychologists call an *internal locus of control*. 'Locus of control' refers to the extent to which people feel that they have control over the events that influence their lives.

People with an *external locus of control* tend to believe that outcomes are the result of their environment or their circumstances – it was 'luck' or 'fate'. Because they believe that they have little power over or influence on their successes or failures, they are more likely to experience anxiety, as they feel that they are not in control of their lives. An external locus of control also creates lower levels of accountability and makes us fragile in the face of change, uncertainty and disruption.

By contrast, people with an *internal locus of control* attribute outcomes to their own efforts and abilities. They understand that, to a large extent, their actions and decisions determine their own successes and failures. This leads to higher levels of accountability, as people with this Own It! mindset are more likely to take responsibility for the consequences of their actions and to be resilient in the face of uncertainty and change.

You'll know whether you're dealing with someone with an external or internal locus of control by the language they use. Someone with a strong internal locus of control will use the word 'I' more often when they talk about what has contributed to the situation or outcome, whether it's good or bad. Those people with an external locus of control, meanwhile, will more often refer to other people or circumstances that are beyond their control.

As with many things in psychology, it's not simply the case that an internal locus of control is 'good' and an external locus of control is 'bad'. But even though there are many variables at play in each, research does suggest that people with a stronger internal locus of control tend to be more achievement-oriented and, as a result, get better-paying jobs. And, in terms of fostering an Own It! mindset, this internal locus of control is critical.

You'll remember that in Chapter 5, we talked about the difference between fruitful accountability relationships (secure, based on trust) and barren accountability relationships (insecure, based in fear). Fostering an Own It! mindset is what helps us move towards the former:

- It gives us the courage to call out those situations in which we have too much to do and too little time and resources to accomplish what we're being asked to deliver on;

- It compels us to own our missteps and mistakes rather than hiding them, so that they can be dealt with effectively; and

- It equips us with the confidence to take responsibility for what's ours to own in our performance and in our accountability relationships.

So, before we ask others to step into their Own It! mindset, we have to make sure we are secure in our own.

Best of all, an Own It! mindset allows us to do all this even when our accountability relationship is edging more towards the barren end of the scale than the fruitful, and is not as safe as we'd like it to be – which, let's be honest, is sometimes (perhaps even often) the case in workplaces.

But in either case, as I've said before, it starts with you.

IT STARTS WITH YOU

There are two reasons why we need to do the work to ensure that we are secure in our Own It! mindset before we ask others to step into theirs.

Firstly, having this mindset ourselves will make it easier to create clarity of accountability expectations (Chapter 4) and assure the quality of our accountability relationships (Chapter 5). Secondly, when accountability challenges arise (which we know they will), it can be very easy to slip into naming, blaming and shaming. Having a firm grasp on your Own

It! mindset, even in the heat, emotion and drama of the moment, will help you achieve more-effective accountability outcomes.

An Own It! mindset doesn't always come naturally or easily. In some cases, it involves working against what psychologists call our *explanatory style*. 'Explanatory styles' are the ways in which we explain our circumstances to ourselves; over time, these can form patterns and become our habitual ways of seeing and interpreting the world – our *mindsets* – to the extent that we begin to offer similar explanations for vastly different events.

When it comes to accountability, there are three positions that I commonly see people taking, each of which is related to their own particular mindset. These positions are:

- Them & Theirs
- Me & Mine
- Us & Ours

Let's have a look at what each of these looks like in action.

Them & Theirs

When we assume a Them & Theirs position, our attention is focused outward: we point fingers at others and focus on what we feel they 'should' be doing. This defensive response is based in fear: as we feel a lack of safety, we 'attack', blaming other people for not meeting *our* expectations.

When we are in this position, we ask questions like:

- 'Why aren't others taking responsibility?'
- 'Why aren't others doing more to support me?'
- 'Why aren't others taking action to fix the situation?'

The problem with this mindset is that it does very little to move the situation forward, and also means that we are avoiding taking on the personal responsibility we need to own.

Me & Mine

Our attention is pointed inward in this position, but it is just as unhelpful as the one described above: here, we point the finger at ourselves, focusing on what we 'should' be doing, and the ways in which we feel we are failing.

Like the Them & Theirs position, this is also a defensive response based in fear. We feel that we are 'not showing up', not meeting the expectations that we have placed on ourselves or that we feel others have of us, and this causes us to direct the 'attack' inwards.

When we are in this position, we think things like:

- 'I should be taking more responsibility.'
- 'I should be doing more to support others.'
- 'I should be taking action to fix the situation.'

The problem with this mindset is that it creates feelings of overwhelm and obligation, and is bounded by the energy, motivation and knowledge of one person – you.

You'll notice that 'name, blame and shame' factors into both of these mindsets – it's just directed at others in the first instance, and at ourselves in the second.

Us & Ours

When we recognise our temptation to point the 'should' finger either outwards or inwards, and understand how this does not lead to the positive, purposeful progress that we want, we can consciously move ourselves toward a third position: that of Us & Ours.

This position is one that is based in confidence. Unlike the Me & Mine position, it comes from a mindset of ownership, with a focus on what we *can* do rather than what we feel we 'should' be doing.

In this position, we ask ourselves questions like these:

- 'What is mine to own in this situation?'
- 'What can I do to help resolve this issue?'
- 'What actions am I able to take to improve the situation?'

From this position of confidence and ownership, we also revisit the contributions that others *could* make to the situation, rather than the 'should'-based expectations of the Them & Theirs position.

When we are in the Us & Ours position, we ask:

- 'What is for others to own in this situation?'
- 'What could others do to help resolve this issue?'
- 'What actions could others take?'

These questions create an *invitation* for others to be involved in the accountability situation, without any expectations of how they 'should' do it.

Us & Ours is the Own It! mindset.

Once we have answered these questions of ourselves and of others, we can open a dialogue with others involved in the accountability situation from the basis of a solution-oriented, Own It! mindset rather than one of 'name, blame and shame'.

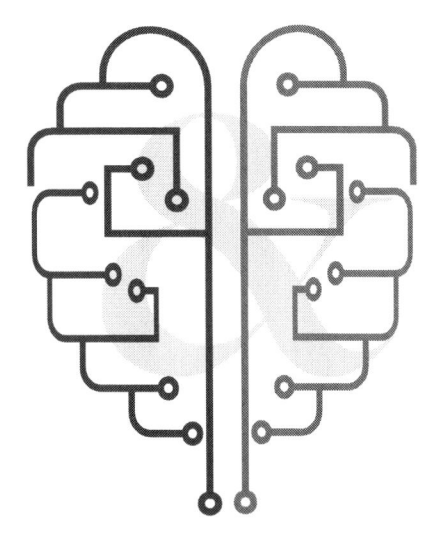

INVITATION

Boundary-Based

Focused on what
others could do

- What is for others to own in this situation?
- What could others do to help resolve this issue?
- What actions are others able to take?

OWNERSHIP

Confidence-Based

Focused on what
I *can* do

- What is mine to own in this situation?
- What can I do to help resolve this issue?
- What actions am I able to take to improve the situation?

Figure 6.1: The Own It! mindset

OWN IT! IN THE REAL WORLD

It's one thing to understand these questions, and another to use them in the day-to-day reality of workplaces. I've found the 'Choice Points' framework, developed by Ann Bailey, Joseph Ciarrochi and Russ Harris for their 2013 book *The Weight Escape*, to be a useful tool to help me foster my Own It! mindset. Choice Points help us to be intentional about who we want to be and how we want to show up by identifying points when we can move towards or away from it.

When things are going well and life is giving us what we want, it's usually fairly easy for us to choose 'towards moves': to act effectively, to treat ourselves and others in ways that create secure relationships, and to do the things that make life better in the long term rather than worse.

But we know that life isn't that easy much of the time, and it doesn't give us what we want for very long. So as challenging situations and difficult thoughts and feelings arise, it's all too tempting to slip into Them & Theirs or Me & Mine positions. This pulls us off track, away from who we want and need to be. Bailey, Ciarrochi and Harris even suggest that almost every psychological disorder, from stress and anxiety to depression and addiction, boils down to this basic process: we get 'hooked' by difficult thoughts and feelings, and begin to make 'away moves'.

Choice Points help us identify the things we do that move us towards the life we want to live and the person we want to be ('towards moves') and the things that we do that move us away from the life we want to live and the person we want to be ('away moves').

However, if we can catch these thoughts running through our minds – what's playing on our 'internal radio' – it is possible to unhook ourselves from these thoughts and feelings. With this awareness, we can choose to make 'towards moves' instead by doing things that move us towards the life we want to live and the person we want to be.

So when I'm in challenging situations and I notice that the 'should' finger inside my head is either pointing at others (Them & Theirs) or at myself (Me & Mine), I understand that there's a choice for me to make: am I going to stay hooked? Or will I unhook and step into my Own It! mindset?

As I mentioned earlier, the 'name, blame and shame' patterns that come with the Them & Theirs and Me & Mine positions have been built up over long periods of time, so it may be that your default setting is to get hooked and do 'away moves'. But as we develop awareness of our patterns, and we are clear about why fostering an Own It! mindset matters to the quality of accountability relationships and outcomes, we find we have a lot more choice about how we respond, and it gets easier for us to make 'towards moves'.

By moving from fear to confidence, from Them & Theirs to Us & Ours and from obligation to invitation, we generate a space in which next steps, actions and accountabilities can be co-created together. We gain clarity about where we need to lean in because something is ours to own, and what we can loosen our grip on or let go of because the ownership rightly sits elsewhere. The outcome is less stress, less drama, less wasted energy, better-quality relationships, and more effective actions and outcomes.

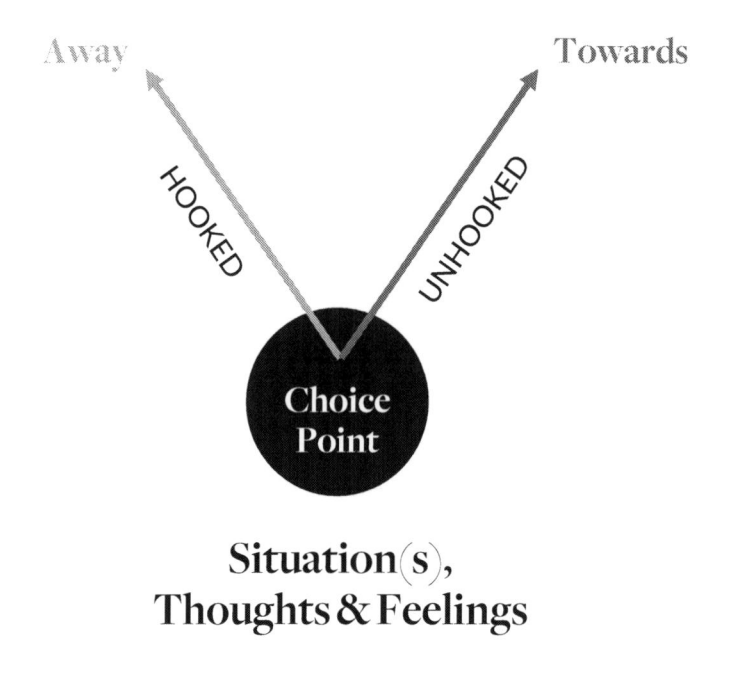

Figure 6.2: Using Choice Points to move towards an Own It! mindset

SUMMARY

» *Mindsets dictate how we see and interpret the world, which in turn shapes how we think, feel, show up and behave.*

» *People who don't have a mindset for accountability – an Own It! mindset – suck us dry of time, energy and attention, present problems rather than solutions, and keep us from making positive, purposeful progress.*

» *People who have an Own It! mindset have an* **internal locus of control**, *which means they feel that their actions are the primary determinants of any given outcome, whether successful or unsuccessful – this has a positive impact on accountability, as they take responsibility for the consequences of their actions.*

» *There are three common positions that people take in relation to accountability:*

- *Them & Theirs*
- *Me & Mine*
- *Us & Ours*

Them & Theirs and Me & Mine are based in fear, while Us & Ours is based in confidence – this latter position is the Own It! mindset.

» *In the Own It! mindset, we ask ourselves:*

- *What is mine to own in this situation?*
- *What can I do to help resolve this issue?*
- *What actions am I able to take to improve the situation?*

And we ask of others:

- *What is for others to own in this situation?*
- *What could others do to help resolve this issue?*
- *What actions could others take?*

These questions provide the basis to open a dialogue with others involved in the accountability situation from the basis of a solution-oriented, Own It! mindset rather than one of 'name, blame and shame'.

» *When in challenging situations or experiencing fear-based thoughts and feelings, being able to identify 'Choice Points' lets us make 'towards moves' in the direction of the person we want to be – the person with the Own It! mindset – rather than 'away moves' that lead us back to the Them & Theirs or Me & Mine positions.*

FROM IDEAS TO ACTION

- Reflect on some of the accountability challenges you have had at work.
  - » What were the language and phrases that were playing on your 'internal radio' when you were in these situations?
  - » Do you recognise a Me & Mine or Them & Theirs pattern in any of the thoughts you had at those times?

- Now think about a recent accountability challenge.
  - » If you had approached it with an Own It! mindset by asking and answering the six Us & Ours questions, what might have been possible that wasn't before?
  - » What would you have done differently?

References

'**Accountability is not just a question of nature or nurture. Accountability is a mindset that can be developed...**' Wakeman, C. (2017). *No Ego: How Leaders Can Cut Workplace Drama, End Entitlement and Drive Big Results.* St. Martin's Press.

'**Neuroscientists have identified mindsets as long-range neural connections...**' Gottfredson, R. (2020). *Success Mindsets: Your Keys to Unlocking Greater Success in Your Life, Work, & Leadership.* Morgan James Publishing.

'**"Locus of control" refers to the extent to which people feel that they have control over the events that influence their lives...**' Rotter, J. C. (1966). *Locus of Control: Current Trends in Theory and Research.* Wiley Press.

'**They are more likely to experience anxiety, as they feel that they are not in control of their lives...**' Pittman, N. L. & Pittman, T. S. (1979). Effects of amount of helplessness training and internal–external locus of control on mood and performance. *Journal of Personality and Social Psychology, 37*(1), 39.

'**They understand that, to a large extent, their actions and decisions determine their own successes and failures...**' Pittman, N. L. & Pittman, T. S. (1979). Effects of amount of helplessness training and internal–external locus of control on mood and performance. *Journal of Personality and Social Psychology, 37*(1), 39.

'**Research does tend to suggest that people with a stronger internal locus of control tend to be more achievement-oriented and, as a result, get better-paying jobs...**' Zhou, W., Guan, Y., Xin, L., Mak, M. C. K. & Deng, Y. (2016). Career success criteria and locus of control as indicators of adaptive readiness in the career adaptation model. *Journal of Vocational Behavior, 94,* 124-130.

'**In some cases, it involves working against what psychologists call our explanatory style...**' Buchanan, G. M., Seligman, M. E. & Seligman, M. (Eds.) (2013). *Explanatory Style.* Routledge.

7.

CAN YOU COACH IT? (PART 1)

SETTING UP FOR SUCCESS

Drama is everywhere. Watercooler gossip, blaming others or circumstances for a lack of results, venting and complaining about non-negotiables, filling information gaps with guesses rather than finding out the facts, defensiveness to feedback, lack of buy-in to team strategies… drama, drama, drama.

As she detailed in her book *No Ego: How Leaders Can Cut the Cost of Workplace Drama, End Entitlement, and Drive Big Results*, workplace researcher Cy Wakeman found that on average, leaders spend two-and-a-half hours each day dealing with these kinds of behaviours, 23% of which had to do with increasing accountability. Can you imagine how much time, energy and money this is wasting in your organisation in a year?

Although many organisations focus on employee engagement as a key driver for performance, Wakeman's research shows that it is accountability rather than engagement that drives business success.

That's worth repeating: It is accountability rather than engagement that drives business success.

This is because engagement is not 'the thing'. Business success – in whatever way that is defined for your team or organisation – is what we're aiming for. Engagement is invaluable, so long as it drives that success. But, despite the fact that organisations spend a lot of time, effort and energy compiling and analysing feedback from employee engagement surveys, that's often not the case.

Why? Because ultimately, engagement is a *choice* – a choice for each individual. It is not something that leaders can 'do and deliver' for their teams by creating the perfect environment for each of them to feel engaged. In fact, Wakeman suggests (and I agree) that *engagement without accountability creates entitlement*.

If your organisation is focusing on engagement, you need to understand that not all the voices in the feedback from your surveys should be weighted equally. The strategic driver to improving performance is to listen to the people who are 'highly accountable' – those who are prepared to get in the arena, try new things, take responsibility for the outcomes and learn forward – rather than those who simply want to heckle from the grandstand. I recently shared this insight with a CEO who I have been mentoring, and it transformed his understanding of the results from his organisation's latest staff survey.

The reality is that it's impossible for organisations to meet the needs of both high- and low-accountability team members. Instead, you should:

Focus on supporting those people with higher accountability and finding ways to coach up the accountability of other team members – or let them go.

LETTING GO TO ASK MORE

We've established that it is accountability, not engagement, that drives results. But to get accountability, you first need to provide *autonomy*.

Autonomy is the need to direct your own life and work. Researchers have found that cultures that provide 'autonomy support' give people the freedom to align what they do, how they do it, when they do it and with whom, with their individual talents and abilities in ways that leave them feeling energised and satisfied. And naturally, the same principle extends to the workplace: in his book *Drive: The Surprising Truth About What Motivates Us*, Daniel Pink proposes that autonomy inspires us to think creatively without needing to conform to strict workplace rules.

Ironically, by letting go of traditional ideas of control and allowing for greater staff autonomy, organisations can ask more of their workers, as they have built trust and improved innovation and creativity – all of which are critical in the increasingly competitive and complex environments in which we operate.

And this shift isn't just useful, it's necessary. In the post-pandemic work world, many of those traditional ideas of control have already had to be let go – things like regular office hours or locations, dress codes, and purely quantifiable targets that don't take account of critical performance indicators such as staff wellbeing.

All of this is why, for Accountors, *coaching* rather than *controlling* – letting go of how you think a task 'should' be done and giving the Accountee the autonomy to approach it in their own way – is the winning strategy. As you can imagine, 'letting go' can feel counterintuitive for many Accountors, who fear that if they give people autonomy, accountability will be shirked and responsibility abandoned. The consequence of this thinking, though, is that many succumb to outdated modes of micromanagement, which leaves people demotivated, disengaged, and condemned to a cycle of underperformance.

This is because when we try to enforce control over people's behaviours, we unintentionally strip away their sense of accountability. Multiple studies have found that when people are provided with autonomy-supportive environments, their desire for connection and a shared sense of purpose means they *willingly* choose to work in ways that are accountable. Accountability thus emerges naturally, rather than having to be forced or imposed.

Allowing for autonomy is also a key part of that fundamental shift we want to make from *holding* people to account to *calling* them to account. Why? Because creating an autonomy-supportive context shifts the function of Accountors from planning and controlling to creating psychologically safe spaces in which Accountees can co-create, self-prioritise, and perform meaningful actions that enable their learning and growth. As Herminia Ibarra and Anne Scoular suggest in an award-winning article for the *Harvard Business Review*: '[Leaders] need to reinvent themselves as coaches whose job it is to draw energy, creativity, and learning out of the people with whom they work.'

Therefore, to be successful as Accountors, we need to move from the role of Controller to that of Coach.

FROM CONTROLLER TO COACH

Once we learn how to coach people to unleash their curiosity, creativity and confidence, we realise how doing so moves us beyond just getting short-term compliance to attaining long-term commitment. These are the secure and fruitful accountability relationships that we talked about in Chapter 5.

Unfortunately, the fact is that most of us don't know how to safely and effectively harness people's neurological, psychological and social strengths through coaching. A study of more than 3,761 executives found that 24% of them significantly overestimated their abilities when their self-assessment of their coaching skills was compared with the experiences of those they coached.

Coaching well can be hard for even the most capable and well-intended, because this approach to accountability changes the way we interact with people. It asks us to prioritise and commit to shaping our interactions in ways that will bring out the best in others and help them to learn, grow and perform, even as we ask them to be accountable for their actions and outcomes.

The good news is that with the right tools and support, and lots of practice and feedback, almost anyone can become a better coach. An effective Accountor-as-Coach consciously adopts their Own It! mindset by:

- Asking questions of their Accountees instead of providing answers,
- Supporting Accountees instead of judging them, and
- Facilitating their development instead of dictating what has to be done.

That first thing especially can feel uncomfortable to begin with, because we live in a world that requires answers – but rarely do we pause to consider what it is we're answering. For many of us, simple questions like 'Why?' can feel like a hindrance to progress, an inefficiency in the face of our constant and anxious drive to act.

But the truth is that change begins not with the actions we take but with the questions we ask, because every action should be preceded by a question. So it is our questions that shape the direction in which our energy, attention and actions grow.

And these aren't just any old questions I'm talking about – oh no!! As David Cooperrider's research into 'Appreciative Inquiry' has shown, 'human systems grow in the direction of their persistent inquiries, and this propensity is strongest and most sustainable when the means and ends of inquiry are positively correlated'. So that means that if we are taking a proper coaching approach to accountability, we need to craft questions that will help generate insight, learning and action.

I can already hear you asking (maybe with a bit of frustration): *'What* questions, Paige?' Don't worry – we'll be covering these in detail later in this chapter and into the next. But first, we need to identify the broad topics that these questions will address.

Research has shown that there are five factors that influence a person's perceived accountability, and as a result impact accountability success. These are:

1. **Attribution** – Will others know it was mine to do?
2. **Observability** – Will others see me doing/not doing it?
3. **Evaluability** – Will I be judged on my actions?
4. **Answerability** – Will I be asked to justify my actions?
5. **Consequentiality** – Will I be rewarded or punished from the result of my actions?

It's important to note that *our perceived accountability is an 'additive function' of all five factors*. This means that when more of these factors are present in an accountability situation, the Accountee will perceive a greater degree of accountability. Unfortunately, we are too often preoccupied with the final factor alone – that of rewards or punishments, which activates our brain's survival instinct.

Understanding the five factors that influence perceived accountability provides us with valuable leverage points as we have conversations that set up, manage and respond to accountability.

This is why our accountability coaching, and the questions we devise as a crucial part of it, need to touch on *all* of these factors – when we go beyond just consequentiality, we have four other leverage points available to us to help us shift accountability in the right direction.

THE DYNAMICS OF THE ACCOUNTABILITY SYSTEM: THE SET-UP, THE EXCHANGE AND THE RESPONSE

We presented the concept of the Accountability System in the introduction to Part III above, where we noted that the component parts of the system are the Accountee, the Accountor, the Accountability Task, and the Accountability Context. As with any system, these elements interact with each other and, at three critical points in these interactions, we are presented with coaching opportunities that can make or break accountability.

These points are:

- the **Accountability Set-up** – the *time* at which the Accountee and Accountor perceive, understand and negotiate accountability expectations,

- the **Accountability Exchange** – the *relationship* between Accountor and Accountee as the accountability task is being undertaken, and

- the **Accountability Response** – the *specific situation* in which the Accountee is called to account by the Accountor.

We're going to look at what coaching for accountability looks like at each of these points. In this chapter, we'll take a closer look at the first stage – the *Accountability Set-up* – from both an Accountor and Accountee perspective. In the next chapter, we'll move on to the *Accountability Exchange* and the *Accountability Response*, so we can learn how we can redirect accountability when it's not quite going to plan!

THE ACCOUNTABILITY SET-UP: THE FIRST CONVERSATION

There are times when we are in the luxurious position of being able to set up accountability expectations and relationships from a clear and clean base. It may be a new team member, a new project, or perhaps just a 'new-to-you' accountability relationship. Whatever the case, the first conversations we have about accountability can go a long way to ensuring success.

As the Accountor, our first job is to make sure that we're in our Own It! mindset and keeping tuned into our internal radio to make sure that the Them & Theirs or Me & Mine mindsets don't move us away from who we want and need to be in this conversation.

Remember, this is about coaching rather than controlling, which means that we need to lead with *questions*. This doesn't mean that we must simply accept the answers the Accountee offers, but it does mean that we are opening a dialogue in which the Accountee leads – a bit like leading on the dance floor. Opening with questions also provides us with insight into the Accountee's current level of understanding about their accountability expectations and consequences.

There are four aspects to the Accountability Set-up conversation that help to ensure that the five success factors for perceived and felt accountability – Attribution, Observability, Evaluability, Answerability and Consequentiality – are present. They are:

1. Establish clear expectations
2. Explicitly ask for accountability
3. Intentionally measure progress and provide support
4. Make clear the visible and undiluted consequences of meeting and missing expectations

Figure 7.2 that follows shows a series of questions in a coaching ladder that you could use for these four stages in the Accountability Set-up conversation.

Establish clear expectations

The purpose of these questions is to reach agreement about the Six

Ws of the accountability task: the Who, What, When, Where, How and Why. Talking about the desired success at different levels (individual, team, organisation) provides a wider context and understanding of why the work under discussion is needed, and how this accountability connects to a wider network of accountability. This is useful for when the conversation turns to consequences later on.

Explicitly ask for accountability

When I work with leaders on accountability, these are the questions that surprise them the most. And yet it's pretty obvious, isn't it – we need to actually *ask* for accountability!

There are a few points to bear in mind here. Firstly, the degree of 'truth' that you'll be given from the Accountee at this point will depend on the level of safety in your accountability relationship (see Chapter 5). Before you ask these questions, it's important to explain that there are no right or wrong answers – the only thing you're looking for is an honest reflection of how the Accountee feels about what you've just discussed.

If, after assuring them of this, you still feel that you're being given the answer the Accountee thinks you *want* to hear, let them know that you would rather understand and work with the reality of their feelings so that you can provide support and remove the possibility of any nasty surprises down the track.

Scaling questions, in which you ask the Accountee to assign their answers a value from 0 to 10, are particularly useful for this kind of discussion. If they give you a lower score on the scale for one of your questions, you can then ask, 'What would need to change for that score to move up by one point, or even just a half?' This opens a dialogue about possible small changes that could make a significant difference in the Accountee's motivation and commitment to the task.

And make sure that you don't just ask it once. Once you have the first answer, follow it up with what coaching expert Michael Bungay Stanier

Clear Expectations

What does success look like - for you, for me, for us? How do you want to achieve the desired outcome? What timeframe will you work towards? What support and/or whose help could make this possible?

Ask for Accountability

If we use a scale of 0-10 where 0 is 'not at all' and 10, is 'very much', how committed/motivated do you feel to make this possible/move forward?

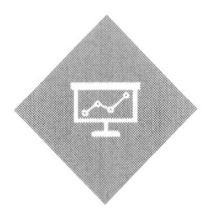

Measure Progress & Provide Support

How can we/do you want to measure progress? How can we measure/do you want to put a spotlight on learning? How often shall we check in?

Visible and Undiluted Consequences

Who is impacted/affected by this work? What are the consequences of this not unfolding as we've planned here?

Figure 7.2: The Accountability Set-up – Coaching Questions Ladder

calls 'the only coaching question you need to know': 'And what else?' By encouraging the Accountee to keep coming up with things that could make a half- to one-point positive difference, you may end up with a number of slight adjustments that, when put together, create a shift of two to three points on the scale. And that will have a significant impact on the success of the accountability task.

Finally come the questions about *commitment* and *motivation*, which should deliberately be kept separate. This is because it's quite rare that we love *every* part of our work responsibilities: there will almost always be some parts of our role that we understand are necessary but, despite our best efforts, we just don't enjoy. Differentiating between commitment and motivation helps us understand and acknowledge how Accountees feel about the various aspects of the task they've been assigned.

If the Accountee gives a higher score for commitment than motivation, this is not a sign that they're stepping out of their Own It! mindset – quite the opposite. They're telling you that they know they need to do this work, even though they don't enjoy it. In addition to the 'What would need to change?' questions above, this can be a good time to explore if anyone else on the team enjoys doing that particular aspect of the task more, and so would have a better experience with it – and, as a result, likely produce a better outcome.

If there isn't any way to either improve or divert the task for the Accountee, then at the very least you, as Accountor, have the understanding that the Accountee is committed to doing work they don't enjoy in order to meet their responsibilities. This gives you the opportunity to provide support and 'cheerlead' as they set about the task.

Intentionally measure progress and provide support

The questions you ask at this stage of the coaching ladder can address a number of the five success factors for perceived and felt accountability. While the goal is still to equip the Accountee with a sense of autonomy over their accountability task, when designed well, progress check-ins, measurement and support can address all five factors with ease and grace.

For example, establishing progress updates on the Accountee's task as a standing item on a team meeting agenda addresses all five: attribution (the team will know this is the Accountee's task to do), observability (depending on the nature of the task, the team will know the Accountee should be taking action on it), evaluability (the team will make some assessment based on the progress report), answerability (it is likely that the Accountee will be asked to explain why the task progress is where it is, whether good or bad), and consequentiality (while there will not be any formal rewards or punishments in the team-meeting setting, the consequences of publicly reporting hitting or missing milestones will influence this).

Along with progress measurement, Accountees also need support through one-on-one check-ins with you, the Accountor. These need to be given just as much priority as the progress questions, as it's in these check-in conversations that the accountability relationship will develop and deepen. As Accountor, it's our responsibility to ensure that these check-ins are established and agreed upon.

Make clear the visible and undiluted consequences of meeting/missing expectations

The questions at this stage of the Accountability Set-up conversation bring the fifth success factor – consequentiality – front and centre. As we covered in Chapter 2, one of the reasons accountability is such an effective motivator is because of the social psychological factors at play. Accountees want to protect their self-image, and so look to gain reward and avoid looking bad in social groups through favourable evaluations from others.

This is why identifying who the work impacts and the consequences of it not unfolding as agreed is so important at this stage: it provides the

Accountee with the understanding of how their task fits into a bigger picture, and which members of their group will be impacted as a result of them not meeting the plan.

Remember, though, that these cautions need to come from a place of love and support rather than fear. Rather than being something that is driven by obligation, making consequences clear to the Accountee is an opportunity to emphasise the meaning, purpose and contribution of their task in the broader accountability context.

And if you're an Accountee…

To this point, we've looked at the Accountability Set-up conversation exclusively from the perspective of the Accountor. But remember, the accountability relationship is not a one-way street: the questions that we outlined above can also be posed by the Accountee to the Accountor, in order to gain greater clarity about your accountability expectations and raise concerns if necessary.

The reality is that your Accountor may not know how important this initial conversation is in setting you up for accountability success. If they are not creating a dialogue with you by asking questions along the lines of the examples in Figure 7.2, then, as Accountees, we can use these questions ourselves in order to initiate that dialogue.

For example, if an Accountor dives right into prescribing what needs to be done, by when and by whom, then you could guide them out of the details by asking if it's okay for you to confirm your understanding of the context and purpose of the work, and how it connects with other people/teams before proceeding with the task. Posing the questions in reverse like this helps the Accountee voice their understanding in the guise of 'checking in' with the Accountor, and allows both sides to achieve the same clarity and agreement of expectations as is achieved when the Accountor asks the questions themselves.

SUMMARY

» As Accountors, assuming the role of Coach rather than Controller creates an autonomy-supportive accountability context for Accountees that leads to greater commitment to progress and outcomes.

» A coaching approach to accountability allows us to leverage the five factors that influence perceived accountability and impact accountability success:

1. **Attribution** – Will others know it was mine to do?
2. **Observability** – Will others see me doing/not doing it?
3. **Evaluability** – Will I be judged on my actions?
4. **Answerability** – Will I be asked to justify my actions?
5. **Consequentiality** – Will I be rewarded or punished from the result of my actions?

» There are three critical points that provide coaching opportunities which can make or break accountability:

1. the **Accountability Set-up** – the time at which both Accountee and Accountor perceive, understand and negotiate accountability expectations,
2. the **Accountability Exchange** – the relationship between Accountor and Accountee as the accountability task is being undertaken, and
3. the **Accountability Response** – the specific situation in which an Accountee is called to account by an Accountor.

» There are four aspects to the Accountability Set-up conversation:

1. Establish clear expectations
2. Explicitly ask for accountability
3. Intentionally measure progress and provide support
4. Make clear the visible and undiluted consequences of meeting and missing expectations

FROM IDEAS TO ACTION

- Reflect on an accountability challenge you are currently experiencing, as either an Accountee or Accountor.

Using a scale of 0 to 10, where 0 = not at all and 10 = completely, to what extent:

  » Are there clear and agreed-upon expectations?

  » Have you asked or been asked for accountability?

  » Do you understand how progress will be measured?

  » Are you clear on the support you may need or need to provide?

  » Do you know the consequences of meeting and missing expectations?

TOTAL: /50

- Now, ask the Own It! mindset questions to explore how to move forward:

  » What is mine to own in this situation?

  » What can I do to help resolve this issue?

  » What actions am I able to take to improve the situation?

- And ask of others:

  » What is for others to own in this situation?

  » What could others do to help resolve this issue?

  » What actions could others take?

References

'**In her book** No Ego...' Wakeman, C. (2017). *No Ego: How Leaders Can Cut Workplace Drama, End Entitlement and Drive Big Results.* St. Martin's Press.

'**In his book** Drive...' Pink, D. (2011). *Drive: The Surprising Truth About What Motivates Us.* Penguin Putnam.

'**Multiple studies have found that when people are provided with autonomy-supportive environments**...' Slemp, G. R., Kern, M. L., Patrick, K. J. & Ryan, R. M. (2018). Leader autonomy support in the workplace: A meta-analytic review. *Motivation and Emotion, 42*(5), 706-724.

'**Herminia Ibarra and Anne Scoular suggest**...' Ibarra, H., & Scoular, A. (2019). The leader as coach. *Harvard Business Review, 97*(6), 110-119.

'**A study of more than 3,761 executives found that 24% of them significantly overestimated their abilities**...' Zenger, J. & Folkman, J. (2016). People who think they're great coaches often aren't. *Harvard Business Review.* https://hbr.org/2016/06/people-who-think-theyre-great-coaches-often-arent

'**As David Cooperrider's research into 'Appreciative Inquiry' has shown**...' *What is Appreciative Inquiry?* David Cooperrider and Associates. https://www.david-cooperrider.com/ai-process/

'**Research has shown that there are five factors that influence a person's perceived accountability, and as a result impact accountability success**...' Han, Y. & Perry, J. L. (2020). Conceptual bases of employee accountability: A psychological approach. *Perspectives on Public Management and Governance, 3*(4), 288-304.

8.

CAN YOU COACH IT? (PART 2)

REDIRECTING FOR SUCCESS

In the previous chapter, we looked at what it means to adopt a coaching approach and mindset in the context of the first part of the Accountability System: the *Accountability Set-up*. But as important as it is to try to set up accountability for success right from the beginning, in reality we don't always have a clean sheet of paper to start from. This is why much of the accountability work that is needed in organisations and teams is not as much about setting up, as about *redirecting* current efforts in order to achieve greater success.

So in this chapter, we're going to look at the remaining two parts of the Accountability System, both of which are involved in that process of redirection: the *Accountability Exchange* and the *Accountability Response*. Understanding these concepts will demonstrate how they can be useful in bringing less-than-ideal accountability scenarios back onto the rails.

THE ACCOUNTABILITY EXCHANGE: FROM THE DRAMA TRIANGLE TO THE PROGRESS TRIANGLE

After the Accountability Set-up conversation we outlined in Chapter 7, the ensuing relationship dynamics between the Accountor and

Accountee as the accountability task is being undertaken naturally has an influence on its progress and outcomes. One of the built-in pitfalls in this relationship is that, even when the Accountee has been encouraged to exercise their autonomy in the performance of their task, that autonomy has to a certain extent been *granted* by a figure of authority – the Accountor. And that inherent imbalance of power opens the door to the kind of dysfunctional interactions mapped by the Karpman Drama Triangle.

The Drama Triangle

First described by and named for the psychiatrist Stephen Karpman, the Drama Triangle is a model that describes the reality of day-to-day human dynamics, illustrating the destructive attitudes that people can take on when personal responsibility and power come into conflict. Karpman proposes that there are three shifting but equally negative roles that participants assume in this model, what he calls the 'three faces of drama': *Victim*, *Rescuer* and *Persecutor*.

Let's examine each of these roles in detail:

VICTIM – HELPLESS AND HOPELESS

Positioned at the bottom of the triangle, Victims have an external locus of control (see Chapter 6) and a 'poor me' mindset. They feel oppressed, powerless and ashamed, and seem unable to make decisions, solve problems, take pleasure in life, or achieve insight. The Victim, if not being actively persecuted already, will actually seek out a Persecutor whom they can pin the blame on, as well as a Rescuer who will 'save the day' for them and, in doing so, perpetuate the Victim's disempowerment and negative feelings about themselves and their situation.

Persecutor
Blame & Shame

Rescuer
Save & Serve

The *Drama* Triangle

Victim
Helpless & Hopeless

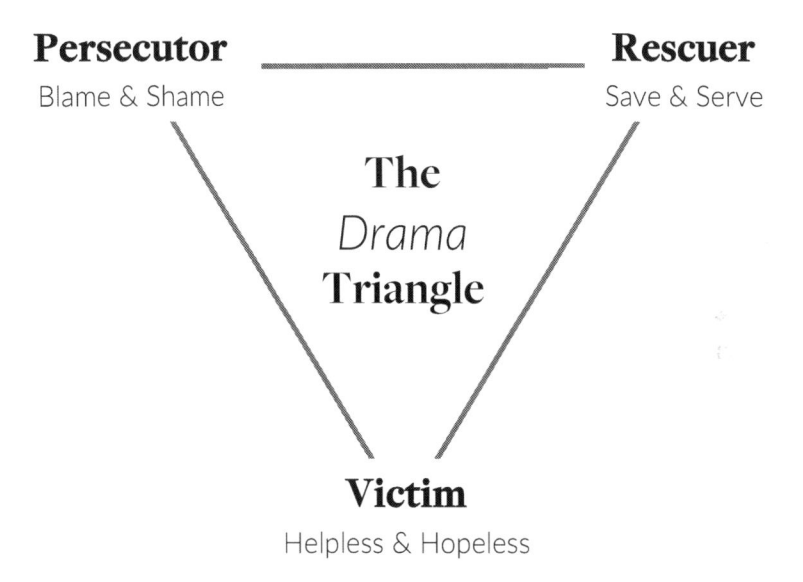

Figure 8.1: The Drama Triangle

RESCUER - SAVE AND SERVE

Rescuers have an overzealous internal locus of control (see Chapter 6) that shows up in a 'let-me-help-you' mindset towards the Victim. The Rescuer feels guilty if they don't rescue the Victim, so much so that they will stretch boundaries by doing more than their share and/or things they don't want to. Their good intentions keep the Victim dependent, and mean that they are not experiencing the consequences of their choices (whether good or bad) and the learning that comes with them.

But why do Rescuers feel compelled to rescue? Precisely to avoid facing their own issues and anxiety by diverting attention and energy to the Victim. Unfortunately, rescuing can be an exhausting pastime, and Rescuers may eventually become resentful of the Victim and withdraw, or move into the role of Persecutor.

PERSECUTOR - NAME AND BLAME

The Persecutor is the 'villain' of the Drama Triangle. Controlling, critical and oppressive, their 'should' finger points squarely at the Victim as they insist that 'It's all your fault.' They act in their own interest and, as the name suggests, look for opportunities to 'punish' others.

As the arrows in Figure 8.1 above suggest, the roles in the Drama Triangle are not fixed: we can move between them multiple times during a drama-filled conversation. However, much in the same way that mindsets are recurring patterns, we can also develop patterns in our interactions over time such that we come to automatically adopt a certain position in the Drama Triangle, regardless of who we are interacting with.

Here's what the Drama Triangle can look like when it comes to accountability:

Accountor: How are things going with the project report? I'll need the complete draft by end of day tomorrow so that I can read it through and let you have my comments before we send it to the client.

Accountee: End of day tomorrow? Well, that's going to be a push with everything else I've got to do. You didn't tell me you needed it then (Victim).

Accountor: Yes I did, in our meeting last week. You know the report has to be with the client by the end of the week. Why haven't you made this a priority? (Persecutor.)

Accountee: When did you tell me? I don't remember that being the deadline. I thought it was next week. I've tried to get the information from the state teams, but they're not getting back to me. There's just no way I'm going to have it done by tomorrow.

Accountor: Who have you been dealing with in each state? Send me through a list of names and I'll contact them to let them know that they have to get the details to you. (Rescuer).

Accountee: Okay, but you should have let me know when this was needed earlier. Now it's just going to make me look stupid in front of them (Persecutor).

Accountor: Well that's not my fault, and there's nothing I can do about it (Victim). The report has to be with the client on Friday, and without the information from the state teams that isn't going to happen. You'll just have to explain that you missed the deadline (Persecutor).

Accountee: Well, that's just great. Thanks a lot, that's really going to help me manage the project moving forward, isn't it? (Victim.)

Do you know someone who is a Rescuer? A Persecutor? A Victim? And more importantly, can you recognise the position you are most likely to adopt?

The Progress Triangle

In the context of accountability, I believe the antidote to the Drama Triangle is the Progress Triangle (Figure 8.2). This model suggests that there are three constructive roles that people play, which, following Karpman's lead, we might think of as being the 'three faces of progress'. These are the *Enabler*, the *Activator* and the *Author*.

As we did for the Drama Triangle, let's take a look at each of the roles of the ProgressTriangle:

AUTHOR - OWN AND ACT

The Author is the opposite of the Victim in the Drama triangle: they have an Own It! mindset and internal locus of control. In taking on personal responsibility, the Author identifies accountability expectations that they can and cannot meet, and, where necessary, will ask for help from a place of invitation – that is, without the belief that the person they are asking *must* provide them with this help.

ENABLER - SUPPORT AND SERVE

Unlike the Rescuer, the Enabler comes from a place of *boundary-based care*. They do not 'push the envelope' of their motivation or ability to support the Author, which means that withdrawal and/or resentment is not a risk. They also do not try to take over and solve the problem for the Author, thereby diminishing and disempowering them. Their focus is not to save, but to *support and serve* towards success – both their own, and the Author's.

ACTIVATOR - PROMPT AND PROPEL

In contrast to the Persecutor, the Activator does not place blame or

Author
Own & Act

The *Progress* **Triangle**

Activator
Prompt & Propel

Enabler
Support & Serve

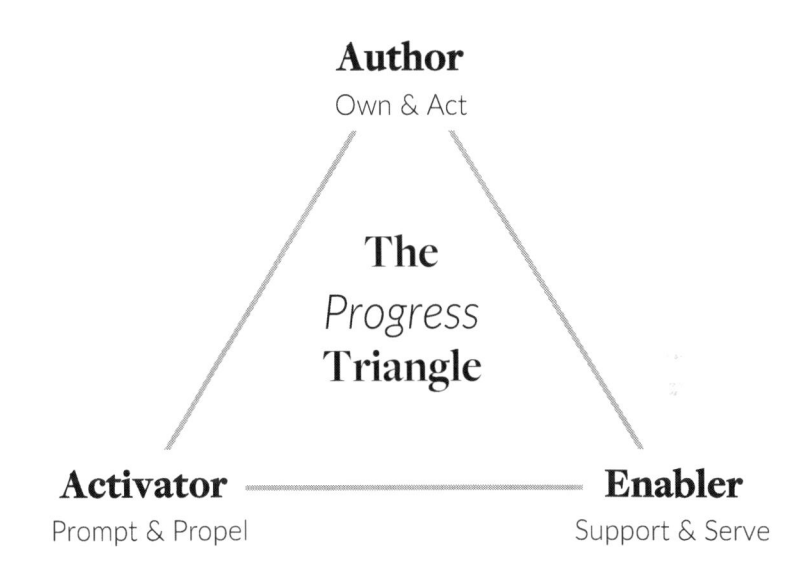

Figure 8.2: The Progress Triangle

punish: they *invite and encourage* the Author to step into their greatness and play a bigger game. They are clear in their own needs and are curious as to the needs of others, which opens a pathway for dialogue and common understanding.

Notice that the Progress Triangle in Figure 8.2 above inverts the orientation of the Drama Triangle. By taking a coaching approach to accountability, we can intentionally engage the Activator and Enabler roles to help move the Accountee from the role of the Victim – who is *held down* at the bottom of the triangle by the actions of the Rescuer and the Persecutor – to that of the Author, who is *supported* at the top by the Enabler and the Activator.

Note also that the arrows on the Progress Triangle diagram are slightly different from those on the Drama Triangle. Here, they all lead to the Author at the top, whereas in the Drama Triangle the participants could potentially shift back and forth between the various roles in an endless cycle.

Let's run through the accountability scenario above again, but this time through the Progress Triangle, with the Accountor taking the role of Enabler and Activator.

> *Accountor:* How are things going with the project report? I'll need the complete draft by end of day tomorrow so that I can read it through and let you have my comments before we send it to the client.
>
> *Accountee:* End of day tomorrow? Well, that's going to be a push with everything else I've got to do. You didn't tell me you needed it then (Victim).
>
> *Accountor:* Yes, remember we discussed it in our meeting last week and agreed that we'd send the report to the client at the end of this week? What else have you got to deliver before end of day tomorrow? (Enabler.)

Accountee: Well, there's nothing by end of day tomorrow, but I have got to get the finance report to the CO by lunchtime the following day, and that's what I was planning on working on tomorrow. Also, I've tried to get the information from the state teams, but they're not getting back to me. There's just no way I'm going to have it done by tomorrow (Victim).

Accountor: Okay, so how about you see if you can have an extra twenty-four hours on the finance report? That's an internal report, so there's likely to be some flex in that deadline. Are you comfortable checking that out? (Activator.)

Accountee: Yes, I can speak to Finance. I don't think they're doing any reporting to the executive on it until next week (Author). But what about the state teams? They're always so slow getting back to me – they just don't see this as a priority (Persecutor).

Accountor: Who have you been dealing with in each state? I wonder if you're connecting with the right people who understand the strategic implications of us not delivering progress reports to the client. Let's go through a list of names together to see if there's anyone else you can connect with to get what you need (Enabler).

Accountee: Okay, I'll print that off now, and then maybe you could send an email with me cc'd to the contacts we decide are the best ones to have going forward, and explain we've got this critical deadline. I could then follow that up with a phone call to each of them this afternoon to talk them through it and establish the ongoing relationship (Author).

Accountor: That sounds great. And let's check in at the end of the day to see how those conversations went and if you need any other targeted support from me (Enabler).

The choices we make for ourselves can have a ripple effect on others, encouraging them to make positive choices for authoring accountability and Own It! for themselves.

When we become aware of Drama Triangle dynamics in regard to accountability expectations, we can intentionally choose to step out of them and into the Progress Triangle roles that support Authoring. Doing so means that we can support others as they work to foster their own Own It! mindset and step into their accountability expectations, whether as an Accountee or Accountor.

THE ACCOUNTABILITY RESPONSE: ASKING THE RIGHT QUESTIONS

The Accountability Response is a specific situation in which an Accountee is being called to account by an Accountor, often because there are issues with accountability expectations not being met. Because of this, we're going to look at this concept primarily through the viewpoint of the Accountor.

Once again, as Accountor our first priority is to ensure we are in our Own It! mindset throughout this conversation, so that we stay out of Them & Theirs or Me & Mine mindsets that could land us in the Drama Triangle.

The Accountability Response conversation has four of the same topic areas as those in the Accountability Set-up conversation that we discussed in Chapter 7. However, in this case there is an additional topic at the very beginning that connects and bridges the two conversations, or re-establishes the accountability agenda if a Set-up conversation has not been held.

The five areas are:

1. Reconnect and make explicit
2. Establish clear expectations
3. Explicitly ask for accountability
4. Intentionally measure progress and provide support
5. Make visible and undiluted consequences clear

Remember, even though we are having this conversation because things have 'gone south' to some degree, we are still in coaching mode here: we are *calling* rather than *holding* the Accountee to account. So, once again, we lead with questions in order to invite the Accountee's autonomy, encourage their personal ownership of the task, and gain insight into their current level of understanding of their accountability expectations.

Figure 8.3 shows the questions and coaching ladder for the five discussion areas in an Accountability Response conversation.

Reconnect and make explicit

The purpose of these questions is to re-establish clarity about the accountability agenda and expectations by reiterating the context and purpose of the Accountability Task. Gaps in the Accountee's knowledge and understanding here may explain why expectations are not being met – for example, perhaps they didn't realise the flow-on effects of not meeting a time deadline, or how their task needs to coordinate with another team member or department.

Whether you are Accountor or Accountee, if there are gaps in your understanding of context and purpose for the accountability task even after an Accountability Set-up conversation has taken place, it's time to lean into your Own It! mindset and check in with what's yours to own in this matter.

> **As Accountor, did you check on the Accountee's understanding by asking enough questions, and really listening to what they said in response?**

> **As Accountee, did you ask enough questions to provide you with the level of clarity and understanding you needed to fulfil your accountability expectations?**

Once we have reconnected with the context and purpose of the accountability task, we move to calling the Accountee to personal ownership in terms of the progress made, their role in the situation, and what they have done to help/hinder progress to the current outcomes.

While this helps the Accountor to understand whether the Accountee has the same perspective on the current situation as they do, it may feel challenging for the Accountee, who may respond defensively by moving into one of the roles in the Drama Triangle. As Accountors, we need to create a psychologically safe space for the Accountee while not backing away from the uncomfortable truths that need to be faced and addressed. This brings us back to the secure, fruitful accountability relationship we discussed in Chapter 5.

If we are the Accountor, reinforce with the Accountee that the purpose of the conversation is to agree on how positive progress can be made with the accountability task, rather than to name, blame or shame; assuming the roles of Enabler and/or Activator can help with this. If we are the Accountee, digging deep into our Own It! mindset and using the questions to discern what is ours to own, and what we can invite the Accountor or others to own or provide support with, will help us get the most out of the conversation.

The final question in this first area – 'Where are we now?' – provides a launching pad for the rest of the conversation. It is entirely likely that there may have been some emotion and drama in the conversation up to this point, so this final question invites the Accountee and Accountor to step back for a moment and establish the current situation of the accountability task. The Accountor needs to encourage the Accountee to provide a purely *factual* response to this question, leaving out the defensive alibis or bruised feelings that may have emerged previously.

For example, the Accountor might say something like this:

> 'Thank you for explaining what's helped and hindered the outcomes that we currently have; it's been really useful to understand that from your perspective. I think it would be good for

Reconnect & Make Explicit

What have we been working towards? What is the purpose of this? How have we progressed? What was your part in this outcome? What did you do that helped/hindered the outcomes we have? Where are we now?

Clear Expectations

Taking into account where we've been (above), what does success now look like, for you, for me, for us? Is it the same, or have things changed? What might you do to add value here? How might you change your approach to achieve this? What timeframe will you work towards? What support do you need to make this possible?

Ask for Accountability

Based on what we've agreed above, if we use a scale of 0-10, where 0 is 'not at all' and 10 is 'very much', how committed and motivated do you feel to move this forward?

Measure Progress & Provide Support

How can we measure progress now? How can we put a spotlight on learning now? When shall we next check in?

Visible and Undiluted Consequences

What are the consequences of this not unfolding as we've planned here, for you, for me, for us?

Figure 8.3: The Accountability Response – Coaching questions ladder

us now to get a sense of where things are at overall, so can you tell me where we are in terms of the following milestones...'

The goal is that, by the end of this part of the conversation, there is clarity and common understanding (even if there's not 100% agreement) between the Accountee and Accountor over the context and purpose of the accountability task, what's contributed to the current situation, and where things are at now.

At this point, we shift our focus from past/present to the future.

Set clear expectations

As with the Accountability Set-up conversation, at this stage of the Accountability Exchange conversation Accountors need to create a sense of personal responsibility for the Accountee in regards to the accountability expectations by asking them what success looks like in light of the current situation. Discussing success through the individual (Accountee and Accountor), team and organisational perspectives will reinforce the interconnected nature of accountability, and asking how this may have changed in light of the current situation acknowledges that things are not where they were expected or need to be.

The next question – 'How might you add value here?' – invites personal responsibility from the Accountee, while also providing an opportunity for them to highlight personal strengths and a desire to contribute.

Ask for accountability/Measure progress and provide support/ Visible and undiluted consequences

These final three topic areas employ the same questions as the Accountability Set-up conversation, while acknowledging that the accountability context has changed.

It's worth noting that you may not need to ask all of these questions, and there may be other questions that you want to add. The Accountability

Set-up and Accountability Response coaching ladders are there as a framework and guide: the work that you do in making the language yours and editing or adding questions that will work for *your* people in *your* context will make your coaching conversations more powerful and effective.

AND WHAT IF THINGS GO WELL?

Of course, the Accountability Response is not just for when things go wrong! It's equally important to have this conversation in order to celebrate success and gather the learning to be gained from the experiences of both the Accountee and the Accountor.

An effective tool to use for this version of the Accountability Response is the *Learning Loop*, which is based on Kolb's reflective learning cycle. The Learning Loop helps you to identify the learnings that can be gained from previous actions, and apply them to future efforts to make sure we keep improving.

The Learning Loop comprises four stages:

1. **Act** – take action, try new ways of thinking, feeling, or behaving
2. **Assess** – review your efforts, consider what is and isn't working and what you've learned
3. **Adjust** – look for ways to incorporate what you've learned into future actions
4. **Assign** – determine when you'll put that learning into practice

In a positive Accountability Response conversation, the Learning Loop coaching ladder might look like this:

Remember: when the accountability task is done and the outcome is achieved, the learning that we gain (whether as Accountor or Accountee) is the gold we take home each time. It is the gift that keeps on giving.

To build our coaching-for-accountability skills and our Own It! mindsets, the Learning Loop must be repeated over and over in order to wire our neural pathways towards mastery.

Coaching for accountability asks us to prioritise and commit to bringing out the best in others. Its goal is to help them to learn, grow, and perform as we ask them to be accountable for their actions and outcomes.

It helps us move out of the Drama Triangle as we lead with questions and create an autonomy-supportive environment in which people take ownership for their responsibilities and author their accountability journey from a place of clarity and agreed-upon expectations.

Accountors who adopt a coaching approach are able to see who is willing or able to move towards becoming an Author, and those who are not. And, as Accountees, we can 'reverse-coach' Accountors in order to help us become the Author of our own accountability journey.

By tuning into our Own It! mindset, staying out of the Drama Triangle, and using coaching questions as a framework for dialogue, we bring transparency and integrity to the accountability process. This not only leads to better outcomes, but also creates trust and safety in our accountability relationships.

And that's something that will serve us well long after the specific task outcomes are done and dusted.

Act
What was the accountability task?
Why was it needed?

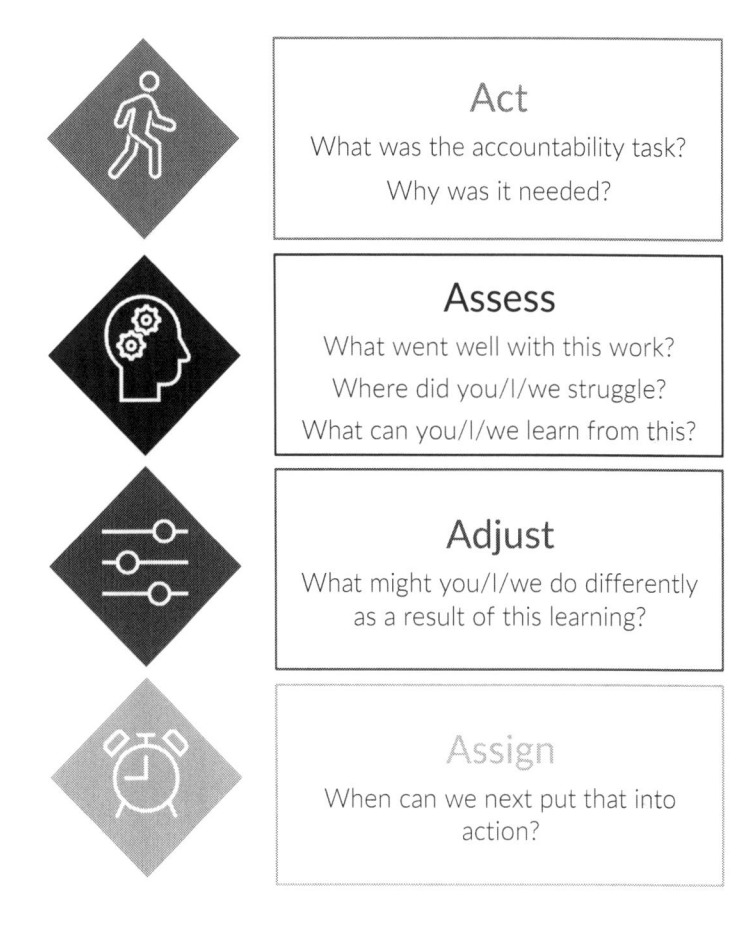

Assess
What went well with this work?
Where did you/I/we struggle?
What can you/I/we learn from this?

Adjust
What might you/I/we do differently as a result of this learning?

Assign
When can we next put that into action?

Figure 8.4: The Learning Loop – Coaching questions ladder

SUMMARY

» The final two critical points in the accountability journey that provide us with coaching opportunities are:

- the **Accountability Exchange** – the relationship between Accountor and Accountee as the accountability task is being undertaken, and

- the **Accountability Response** – the specific situation in which an Accountee is called to account by an Accountor.

» If the Accountor does not adopt a coaching approach during the Accountability Exchange, the relationship between Accountor and Accountee can fall into the destructive pattern of the Drama Triangle, in which people can shift between the equally unhelpful roles of Persecutor, Rescuer and Victim.

» Alternatively, we can choose to move away from these drama-inducing roles and take on the constructive roles of Enabler, Activator or Author within the Progress Triangle.

» The Accountability Response conversation adds one extra topic area before the four areas that were addressed in the Accountability Set-up conversation (see Chapter 7 summary):

1. Reconnect and make explicit

2. Establish clear expectations

3. Explicitly ask for accountability

4. Intentionally measure progress and provide support

5. Make visible and undiluted consequences clear

» In the event of a positive Accountability Response conversation, we can focus on celebrating success and gathering the learning gained by using the three stages of the Learning Loop:

1. **Act** – take action, try new ways of thinking, feeling or behaving

2. ***Assess*** *- review your efforts, consider what is and isn't working and what you've learned*

3. ***Adjust*** *- look for ways to incorporate what you've learned into future actions*

» *Accountors who adopt a coaching approach are able to see who is willing or able to move towards becoming an Author and who is not.*

» *Accountees can apply the same coaching principles in order to 'reverse-coach' Accountors in order to help them become the Authors of their own accountability journey.*

FROM IDEAS TO ACTION

- Without judgement, reflect on a time that you recognise you were in the Drama Triangle in an Accountability Exchange:
    - » What was happening in this moment?
    - » What role(s) did you take?
    - » What impact did this have on you? On others? On the business?
    - » What were the consequences for you? For others? For the business?

References

'**First described by and named for the psychiatrist Stephen Karpman, the Drama Triangle**...' Burgess, R. C. (2005). A model for enhancing individual and organisational learning of 'emotional intelligence': The drama and winner's triangles. *Social Work Education*, 24(1), 97-112.

'**An effective tool to use for this version of the Accountability Response is the Learning Loop**...' Kolb, D. (1984). *Experiential Learning: Experience as the Source of Learning and Development*. Prentice Hall.

9.

WILL YOU CRAFT IT? SHAPING A CULTURE OF ACCOUNTABILITY

RECENTLY, I WAS WORKING WITH THE EXECUTIVE TEAM OF A LARGE insurance firm on resetting accountability. The CEO recognised that the legal imperative for accountability that has changed the face of financial services is barrelling towards the insurance industry, and he was determined to keep his organisation ahead of the wave.

One of the challenges the team was facing was how to make accountability part of the normal way of working across a large and dispersed workforce. It's a problem I see many leaders and organisations are challenged by, particularly as hybrid work becomes more widespread.

There's a saying in the social sciences: 'context is king'. Even though it can be useful to remove 'noise' when you are researching a particular idea or process, the reality is that everything happens in context, and to remove context from the picture makes it less informative, accurate and real – whether it's our current thinking in the context of our previous experiences, team dynamics in the context of the current workload, or individual staff performance in the context of broader influences such as mental and physical health. And the same is true for accountability: just like those other examples, context matters.

This is why my work in creating a consistent approach to accountability across a complex, distributed workforce with this CEO and his organisation focused on creating an Own It! culture. Because intentionally creating a culture of accountability normalises the mindsets, attitudes and behaviours that support Own It! both individually and collectively.

And the good news is, it doesn't need to involve lots more 'to-dos'.

CULTURE EATS STRATEGY...

The saying goes that 'culture eats strategy for breakfast'. This is because workplace and team culture, while invisible, have been shown to be a powerful influence on how things are done in organisations, and, consequently, on what is achieved.

In my experience leading teams and organisations, and in working with leaders and teams across business, education, government and NGOs, I've found that there's a kind of mystique around culture. We know it can make or break the experience of work for people and the outcomes they achieve, but there's also evidence to suggest that culture change is hard at best and impossible at worst.

Leaders have told me that they feel as if culture is always just out of reach. It's like trying to grab smoke – you reach for it, you think you've got it, but when you look in your hand, it's not there. And I know what that's like, because I've felt it as a leader too.

But I've come to realise, through both my research and my professional experience, that the key to being more successful at culture change is to change our thinking about culture. We need to understand it not as something that is separate from leaders, teams or organisations, but as something that is *socially constructed*.

Culture is created by people, through the way that they behave and interact with each other. And that means YOU.

The reality is, we can't help but create culture because it emerges as we learn the most effective ways to organise and coordinate our work together. Culture becomes apparent through the patterns in our interactions and dynamics – it is a *learning process*.

When we look at culture through the lens of learning, we can understand it as the most successful way we have learned to be and do together to achieve the outcomes we want and need. Over time, these ways of being and doing are normalised, and as new members join the culture they recognise that 'This is the way things are done around here,' and adopt those same ways of being and doing. This 'copycatting' process of socialisation is hugely powerful, because it fulfils one of our deepest psychological needs for connection and a very real 'survival' need to be part of the tribe. This also explains how culture embeds and expands, why it stays and sticks, and why it can feel so hard to shift.

In fact, one of the reasons that so much culture-change work has been less than successful is because it's tried to cross too many complex systems and boundaries. Leadership and systems researcher Meg Wheatley suggests that we need to let go of the idea that we can change and transform large, complex systems, and instead focus on creating 'islands of sanity' within our sphere of influence.

I love this! I love the idea that we can each create islands of Own It! and that over time, as more people and leaders do the same, our islands will join up to create larger and larger masses, until we have a whole Own It! continent that looks a bit like a patchwork quilt, with lots of islands joined together.

So what does this mean for creating a culture of accountability?

THE FOUR RS: WORKING WITH WHAT YOU HAVE

If we accept that culture is a learning process, culture expert and researcher Professor Edgar Schein suggests that the first step to creating change is the decision by group members to consciously do something new and different.

The good news about this is that it doesn't have to mean lots of additional work or major transformation. Based on my research, my years of trying to wrangle culture as a leader of teams and organisations, and my work with leaders who are trying to do the same, I've found that using what is already happening in the team or organisational culture is the most effective way to create cultural change.

The existing cultural practices are the most effective way that the group has learned to work together, so, rather than blowing that out of the water, we should identify the strategic leverage points – what I call the 'containers of the culture' – and focus our attention on those.

I've identified four containers that have a particularly dynamic and reinforcing relationship with each other, which makes them the most effective variables to work with when seeking to create change in a cultural system. I call them the *Four Rs*:

1. Role modelling
2. Routines
3. Rituals
4. Rhythms

The Four Rs framework helps us identify how to leverage what is already happening in the group in order to craft the culture we want to create. Let's have a look at what this could look like for an Own It! culture.

Role modelling

For leaders, the emergent quality of culture provides both the greatest opportunity and the greatest challenge. Professor Schein suggests that 'The only thing of real importance that leaders do is create and manage culture.' This is because leaders enjoy a unique position in

Role Model — Behaviours you want others to follow

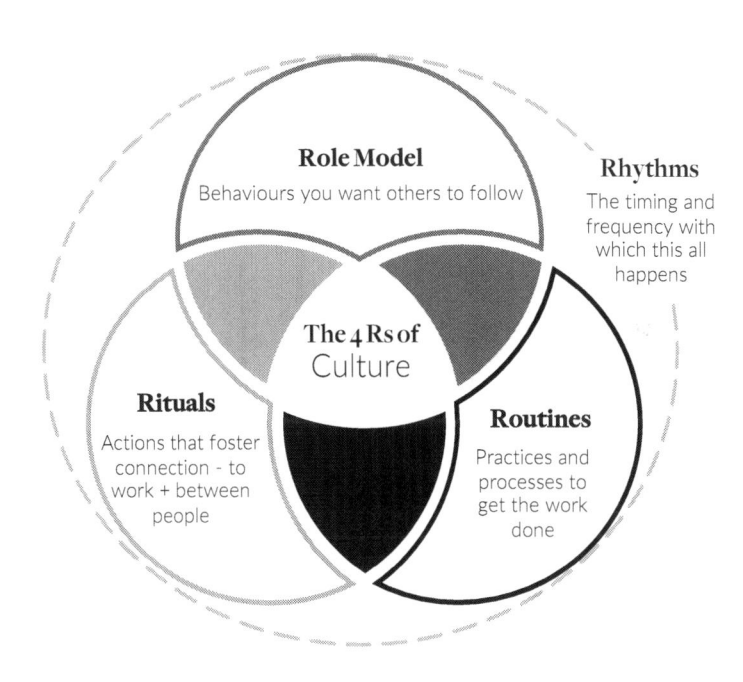

Rhythms — The timing and frequency with which this all happens

Rituals — Actions that foster connection - to work + between people

Routines — Practices and processes to get the work done

The 4 Rs of Culture

Figure 9.1: The Accountability Context: The Four Rs framework

organisations as both consumers and creators of culture. Due to the influence leaders have in directing energy and resources within a team, how they show up and behave and where they focus their attention is a powerful influence in creating team norms. This is why culture change truly begins when leaders start to model the mindsets and behaviours they want their team to emulate.

I'm sure that, like me, you've been in situations where you've been asked to do something differently, but leaders haven't set the example – as if they are in some way exempt from needing to make the change themselves.

Do you remember how disheartening that was? How it made you feel like the change was being done 'to you' rather than 'with you'?

Dialling up accountability is not easy work. There's bound to be discomfort along the way as people make the transition to the 'new normal'. This is why it's critical that we, as culture leaders, step up and lead by example – sharing our discomfort as we do – so that others feel okay to struggle and safe to flag it with us as they go on the journey.

This means we need to take time to consider how we can authentically bring a culture of Own It! to life through our leadership. If you hold a formal leadership role, this means you provide clear expectations to your team about the mindsets and behaviours that you want and need from them, and are consistent in rewarding those behaviours with attention and praise.

The first and most powerful step towards successful culture change is to look in the mirror and make sure you are role modelling the kind of behaviours you want others to follow.

If you're not the formal leader, lean into your informal influence and role model the behaviours that you would *like* your formal leader to be modelling. Remember: each of us can create islands of Own It! through our sphere of influence.

Beyond role modelling, what other levers do we have to influence culture?

Routines

In the same way that individuals have habits and patterns of behaviour, teams have rhythms, rituals and routines to the way they work together. All of these can be used as a helpful scaffolding to support culture-change efforts. Rather than 'adding on' to the way the team works together, we use existing work practices and processes as the 'containers' in which the new or evolving culture is brought to life.

Like knowing the steps to a dance, routines are valuable because they save time and energy by removing the need to think about and coordinate people around every individual task – the team knows the routine, and so can get things done faster. Routines include things like communications processes, team meetings, and performance or project reviews.

I call these the 'mechanics' of a team or group.

Rituals

To understand what I mean by 'rituals' as opposed to routines, imagine for a moment that you're one half of a ballroom-dancing partnership. Rituals are like knowing (and liking!) the personality of your dance partner – your dancing together may be technically perfect, but if it doesn't have that certain *something* in the energy between the partners, it won't have as much impact. Heidi Grant of the NeuroLeadership Institute suggests that rituals help people feel more deeply involved in their team experience, which in turn means they value it more.

Rituals can be work-related – for example, the way in which a new team member is inducted into the team, or your team celebrates mutual success – or personal, such as team-member birthdays or farewells. I think of rituals as the 'social glue' that helps us connect with each other personally, and also to the purpose of our being together – which is often the work we are doing. Rituals support the *dynamics* of a team or group.

Side note: while it's useful for our purposes in this book to separate routines and rituals for the sake of clarity, in reality they may not always happen as separate 'events'. For example, you may find that in a team meeting you shine a light on accountability success (team dynamics = ritual), and also talk about progress on a project (team mechanics = routine).

Rhythms

In the same way that music has a beat that sets the tone of the piece, the rhythm of your culture is about the timing with which role modelling, routines and rituals occur. This is important, because how frequently something occurs sends a signal to the group about how important it is.

Research by the Leaders Lab indicates that unless team members experience something frequently, it really doesn't land in their consciousness and make a difference to their mindsets, attitudes or behaviours. This means that the rhythm with which role modelling, routines and rituals are actioned can make a big difference in the speed of cultural change.

The frequency – or Rhythm – with which you leverage the Four Rs is critical to creating reinforcing dynamics that will normalise and embed an Own It! mindset.

For example, how often do you role model personal ownership? With what frequency do you discuss collective responsibility in team meetings? Are your performance review conversations annual, quarterly, monthly?

The Four Rs: Filling the containers

So, we've now removed some of the mystique that surrounds culture change by understanding it as a *learning process*, and identified the containers that we can use as leverage points to shift the cultural system: the Four Rs of role modelling, routines, rituals and rhythms.

Now that we have our containers, what are we going to fill them with to bring the Own It! culture to life?

When we talk about change, the terms 'top-down' and 'bottom-up' are often used. The former refers to a change agenda that comes from the 'top' of the organisation or system; that is, from the leadership. While there may be consultation along the way, this model is driven by a tell-and-control, plan-and-direct energy. An example of how this works can be seen in Kotter's 8-Step Change Model, in which a compelling platform and plan for change is established by leaders at the 'top', and these are then communicated and cascaded down through the rest of the organisation – for instance, an organisation-wide training program about effective goal-setting may be offered to employees with a directive that everyone has to attend within the next three months in order to support a new performance management system that is being rolled out.

Bottom-up change (sometimes also called 'grassroots' change), as you would guess, comes from the 'bottom' levels of the organisation or system. This kind of change is often not formalised, but rather emerges from a felt need, because current ways of being and doing are no longer optimal to meet what we want and need to do together. For example, a work team may decide to create a 'progress tracker' wall in their workspace or begin their weekly team meetings with progress check-ins, thus changing the physical environment and processes in their team.

One of the challenges with grassroots change is that it can be stifled or rejected by the formal system because it isn't part of a 'legitimate' change agenda. But actually, there's a problem with *each* of these views of change, in that both the top-down and the bottom-up models focus on *where* the change agenda is coming from, which can make change more political than it needs to be. This is because it highlights the endemic power differential in workplace structures, in that levels higher up in the organisation get to set and direct the change agenda.

But by asking and answering a different question, we reduce the power differential and the politics, and can take more-effective action to shift culture.

> **The question we need to ask is:**
>
> *What needs to change for culture to change?*

With our understanding that culture is a learning process, the answer to this question becomes clear: what needs to change is our way of being and doing together to get the work that we want and/or need to do, done.

So the solution to this equation is:

Culture change = Behaviour change

THE BEHAVIOUR CHANGE LOOP

Research into behaviour change has come a long way in the last few decades, thanks to concepts like behavioural economics and 'nudges' from the New Economic Foundation in the UK; the study and popularisation of habits by authors such as Charles Duhigg and James Clear; and the work of Dr B.J. Fogg and his team at the Stanford Behaviour Design Lab.

Bringing together this research with what we know about motivation and sustaining change from psychology and neuroscience, I've found that the simplest way to think about what we want to fill our cultural containers with is to use the *Behaviour Change Loop* (see Figure 9.2). We can use this framework to intentionally design the behaviour change needed to move towards an Own It! culture, as it taps into the way our brains are naturally wired to create change.

This model is composed of three factors:

1. **When…** – a trigger event or time
2. **Then…** – the behaviour or action
3. **So that…** – the purpose or desired outcome

When… (The Prompt)

The first thing our brains need is a prompt to trigger the behaviour – the 'When…'. But remember, this isn't about adding more work to your day, so we need to use the existing routines and rituals in the culture as our 'When…'.

Fogg and other behavioural science researchers suggest that an effective way to create a prompt is to anchor a new habit to an existing, established behaviour or habit. James Clear calls this 'habit-stacking', which is effectively what we're doing. By leveraging what's already going on with our routines and rituals, there are fewer obstacles for change because the prompt is already in place.

Research also suggests that we need to start small, with what Fogg defines as 'tiny habits' and what I like to call '1% behaviours'. Why 1%? Because small changes keep our brain feeling safe, which drives action and builds the momentum we need to approach bigger changes and make quicker progress. A 1% change might feel small, but over time it has a powerful impact: if culture improves by just 1% each day for a year, through the compounding effect over the twelve months it will be 378% better by the end of it. And that's something worth aiming for.

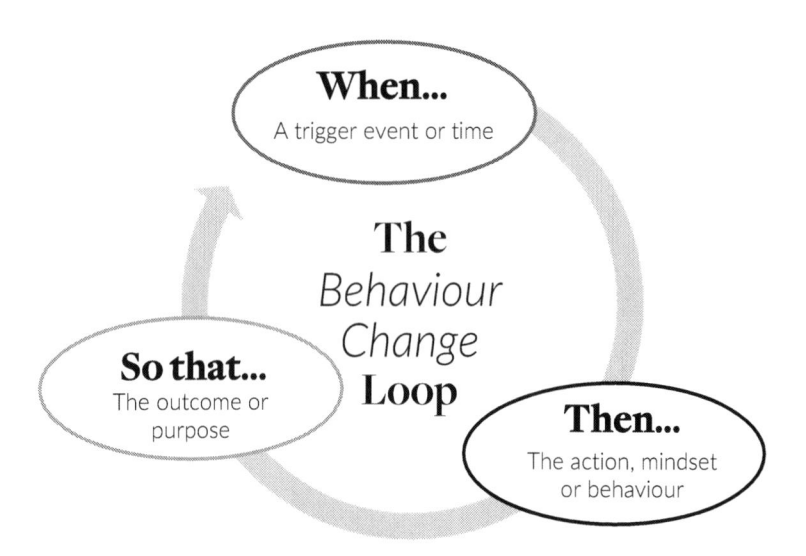

Figure 9.2: The Behaviour Change Loop

Then... (The Action)

Once we have a trigger, we need to identify the accountability behaviours that would help us create an Own It! mindset. This is the 'Then' in the Behaviour Change Loop.

What this looks like will be specific to the people and context you are working with, but a simple way to think about this is to use the well-known 'stop/start/continue' framework. Ask yourself: for there to be more of an Own It! culture in your team, which behaviours would need to stop, which would need to start, and which would you want to continue? You don't need too many of these: it's better to have a few key behaviours that you reinforce through multiple trigger events or times by role modelling, routines and rituals.

Neuroscience tells us that it takes repetition to build new neural pathways towards mastery, and that is true. But in addition to repetition, there is another key element required – positive emotions. Fogg's research found that we only respond reliably to trigger events as prompts when we are motivated and able to do so. Which brings us to the final stage of the Behaviour Change Loop: 'So that...'.

So that... (The Outcome)

With the trigger and behaviour in place, we now consider the reason why we want the behaviours we've identified above – what impact or outcome are we aiming for? This is a check on our rationale, but also a critical component of the brain science behind behaviour change: understanding the purpose of the behaviours and celebrating success when you see them in action lays down memories in your brain that help motivate the behaviour next time the trigger event comes around.

Research shows that learning with an emotional overlay is 'stickier' than learning that is simply fact-based. So if we want to build new behaviours as effectively and sustainably as possible, adding the emotional experience of purpose and success embeds the behavioural and cultural change more quickly.

PUTTING IT ALL TOGETHER

Understanding that culture is a socially constructed learning process helps us see that the decision to make cultural change lies with us and our intentional focus and attention. By using the Four Rs of role modelling, routines, rituals and rhythms, we can identify existing opportunities to intentionally integrate the personal responsibility and shared accountability of an Own It! culture into the ways our teams are already working. And the Behaviour Change Loop provides us with an evidence-based framework that supports us to intentionally consider the When, What and Why as we design and craft the behaviour changes that will enable our desired cultural shifts.

Not only does this save time and energy as you juggle the weight of your existing obligations, but it makes many of the responsibilities you've been struggling to meet much easier and often more joyful to fulfil.

SUMMARY

» Team culture is a powerful influence on how things are done in organisations, and, consequently, on what is achieved.

» Culture is socially constructed in that it is created by people, through the way that they behave and interact with each other. Culture is also a learning process because it emerges as we learn the most effective ways to organise and coordinate our work together to achieve the outcomes we want and need.

» Over time, these ways of being and doing are normalised, which is why culture is also notoriously difficult to change. This is why using what is already happening in the team or organisational culture is the most effective way to create cultural change.

» There are four 'containers of culture' that have a particularly dynamic and reinforcing relationship with each other, which makes them the most effective variables to work with when seeking to create a cultural system. These are known as the Four Rs:

   1. Role modelling
   2. Routines
   3. Rituals
   4. Rhythms

   The Four Rs help us identify how to leverage what is already happening in the group in order to craft the Own It! culture we want to create.

» We can use the Behaviour Change Loop to intentionally design the behaviour change needed to move towards an Own It! culture. The Behaviour Change Loop has three elements:

   1. When… – a trigger event or time
   2. Then… – the behaviour or action
   3. So that… – the purpose or desired outcome

FROM IDEAS TO ACTION

- Think about the current ways of working and being together in your team, and make a note of the rituals and routines that currently exist. Then, think about the behaviours you would like to stop, start and continue in order to bring an Own It! culture to life.

    » As you do this, consider what the specific behaviour would be and in what way it puts an Own It! mindset into action. What would the impact or outcome be of stopping/starting/continuing this behaviour?

- You can now use the Behaviour Change Loop to plan out the cultural change that you want to create through existing routines and rituals.

WHEN (TRIGGER)	THEN (ACTION/BEHAVIOUR)	SO THAT (PURPOSE/IMPACT)
When...	Then I will...	So That...
When...	Then I will...	So That...
When...	Then I will...	So That...
When...	Then I will...	So That...
When...	Then I will...	So That...
When...	Then I will...	So That...

- Now it's time to think about your role as a culture leader.
    - » How can you role model personal ownership and share your struggles and successes with accountability with your team?
    - » Use the Behaviour Change Loop to design the behaviours you will role model to accelerate the culture change that you want to create.

WHEN (TRIGGER)	THEN (ACTION/BEHAVIOUR)	SO THAT (PURPOSE/IMPACT)
When…	Then…	So That…
When…	Then…	So That…
When…	Then…	So That…
When…	Then…	So That…
When…	Then…	So That…
When…	Then…	So That…

References

'**But there's also evidence to suggest that culture change is hard at best and impossible at worst...**' Smith, M. E. (2002). Success rates for different types of organizational change. *Performance Improvement, 41*(1), 26-33.

'**Leadership and systems researcher Meg Wheatley suggests that we need to let go of the idea that we can change and transform large, complex systems...**' Wheatley, M. (2017). *Who Do We Choose to Be? Facing Reality, Claiming Leadership, Restoring Sanity.* Berrett-Koehler.

'**Edgar Schein suggests that the first step to creating change is the decision by group members to consciously do something new and different...**' McQuaid, M. (Host). (2020, December 3). Are you a humble leader? (#215) [Audio podcast episode]. In *Making Positive Psychology Work.* https://www.michellemcquaid.com/podcast/are-you-a-humble-leader-podcast-with-edgar-peter-schein/

'**Professor Schein suggests that "The only thing of real importance that leaders do is create and manage culture"...**' McQuaid, M. (Host). (2020, December 3). Are you a humble leader? (#215) [Audio podcast episode]. In *Making Positive Psychology Work.* https://www.michellemcquaid.com/podcast/are-you-a-humble-leader-podcast-with-edgar-peter-schein/

'**Heidi Grant of the NeuroLeadership Institute suggests that rituals help people feel more deeply involved in their team...**' Grant, H. (2013, December 12). New research: Rituals make us value things more. *Harvard Business Review.* https://hbr.org/2013/12/new-research-rituals-make-us-value-things-more

'**Research by the Leaders Lab indicates that unless team members experience something frequently...**' The Leaders Lab 2021 Workplace Report.

'**An example of how this works can be seen in Kotter's 8-Step Change Model...**' Kotter, J. P. (1995). Leading change: Why transformation efforts fail. *Harvard Business Review, 85*(1), 59-67.

'**Research into behaviour change has come a long way in the last few decades...**' John, P. (2016). Behavioral approaches: How nudges lead to more intelligent policy design. In B. Guy Peters & P. Zittoun (Eds.), *Contemporary Approaches to Public Policy: Theories, Controversies and Perspectives* (pp. 113-131). Palgrave Macmillan.

'**The study and popularisation of habits by authors such as Charles Duhigg and James Clear**…' Duhigg, C. (2013). *The Power of Habit: Why We Do What We Do and How to Change.* Random House; Clear, J. (2018). *Atomic Habits: An Easy & Proven Way to Build Good Habits & Break Bad Ones.* Random House.

'…**and the work of Dr B.J. Fogg and his team at the Stanford Behavior Design Lab**…' Fogg, B. J. (2019). *Tiny Habits: The Small Changes That Change Everything.* Eamon Dolan Books.

'**Research also suggests that we need to start small, with what Fogg defines as "tiny habits" and what I like to call "1% behaviours"**…' Fogg, B. J. (2019). *Tiny Habits: The Small Changes That Change Everything.* Eamon Dolan Books.

'**Neuroscience tells us that it takes repetition to build new neural pathways towards mastery**…' Rock, D. (2009). *Your Brain at Work: Strategies for Overcoming Distraction, Regaining Focus, and Working Smarter All Day Long.* HarperCollins.

'**Research shows that learning with an emotional overlay is "stickier" than learning that is simply fact-based**…' Fogg, B. J. (2019). *Tiny Habits: The Small Changes That Change Everything.* Eamon Dolan Books.

CONCLUSION

AVOIDING THE 'DARK SIDE' OF ACCOUNTABILITY

THROUGHOUT THIS BOOK, WE'VE TALKED A LOT ABOUT ACCOUNTability being the solution to the epidemic of underperformance in organisations.

We've explored how we can reset accountability from a punitive position of *holding* people to account to *calling* them there from a place of love, possibility and an invitation to play a bigger game.

We've looked at the two critical factors that research suggests can help us do this: *clarity of accountability expectations* and the *quality of accountability relationships*.

And we've shown how we can put these ideas into action by adopting an Own It! mindset, coaching for accountability, and intentionally crafting a culture where that Own It! mindset is embedded in the mechanics and dynamics of our teams.

So – where to next?

Well, like many things in life, more is not always better when it comes to accountability. Research has found that there may be a curvilinear relationship between accountability and performance similar to stress, whereby there is a sweet spot, or 'golden mean', that we are looking to sustain.

The figure that follows shows the curvilinear nature of accountability, which suggests that too little or too much impacts performance, progress, and the outcomes we can achieve. This is because accountability can function as both a challenge, which boosts performance, or as a threat, which leads to self-protective behaviour and lower performance.

Under- or *unclear accountability* is what we have been talking about addressing throughout this book to eliminate underperformance. We do this through *activated accountability*, in which we shift from *holding* to account to *calling* to account and improving the clarity of expectations and quality of accountability relationships. This is the sweet spot for the capacity, capability, progress and performance in you, your team and your organisation.

However, it's when we move beyond this that we enter the 'dark side' of accountability. I've seen this show up in two different forms: *over-accountability* and *inappropriate accountability*, both of which have negative consequences, but in slightly different ways. *Over-accountability* is when there are simply too many accountability expectations to be met. *Inappropriate accountability* is when the appropriate resources, knowledge, skills or authority are not available to make it realistic for the expectations to be met.

The negative consequences of over- and/or inappropriate accountability are well-documented, and include increased job stress, emotional exhaustion, and depressed mood. This highlights the importance of knowing your people and paying attention to the stress levels and mental health of yourself, your colleagues and your team.

It also reinforces the importance of assessing the broader Accountability Context, as this is often the critical factor in the specific location of the tipping point from activated accountability to the 'dark side'. For

AVOIDING THE 'DARK SIDE' OF ACCOUNTABILITY

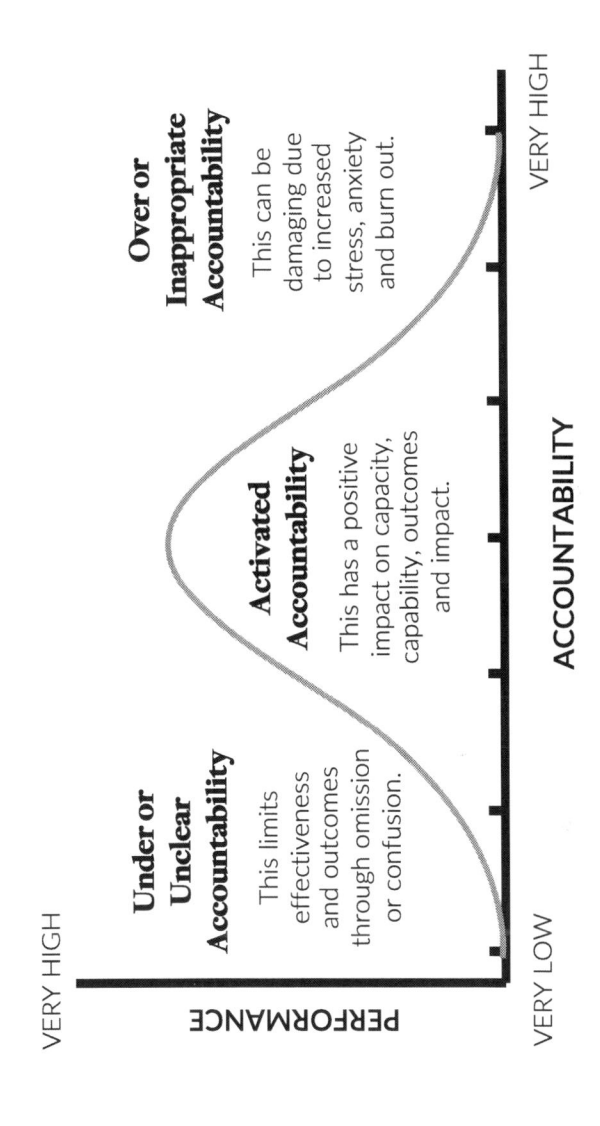

Under or Unclear Accountability
This limits effectiveness and outcomes through omission or confusion.

Activated Accountability
This has a positive impact on capacity, capability, outcomes and impact.

Over or Inappropriate Accountability
This can be damaging due to increased stress, anxiety and burn out.

Figure 10.1: The curvilinear nature of accountability

example, how is the mental health and wellbeing of the individual or team? What influence are the wider organisational structures and culture having? What influence do work practices such as hybrid teams have on the Accountability System that you're working with?

We take a closer look at three contexts that can influence where the tipping point sits in the case studies included in the Appendix. You can find these on page 175.

FINAL WORDS

Own It! is a game changer. I say that with confidence, because I've experienced the difference it's made in my life as I've researched and written this book, and developed and applied the ideas and tools it describes.

Reframing accountability as an act of love has helped me lean into the necessary work of asking for it. Using the Own It! mindset questions has increased my self-confidence in navigating tricky, challenging and complex situations and dynamics in a way that is 'clean' and has no agenda other than purposeful progress. Setting up accountability for success and redirecting it through coaching questions with my team (not to mention my teenage daughters!) has saved time, effort and energy, and reduced drama. And creating it as a cultural norm through my role modelling, and intentionally crafting routines and rituals that ask for and expect it, has made my business hum with productivity.

You can do it too.

It will take time, will feel uncomfortable, and, as with any change, there'll be times when you want to throw in the towel. But I guarantee it will be worth it.

So let me ask you again:
Are you ready to play a bigger game?

References

'**Research has found that there may be a curvilinear relationship between accountability and performance similar to stress...**' Ganster, D. C. & Schaubroeck, J. (1991). Work stress and employee health. *Journal of Management, 17*(2), 235-271.

'**The negative consequences of over- and/or inappropriate accountability are well-documented, and include increased job stress...**' Laird, M. D., Perryman, A. A., Hochwarter, W. A., Ferris, G. R. & Zinko, R. (2009). The moderating effects of personal reputation on accountability-strain relationships. *Journal of Occupational Health Psychology, 14*(1), 70.

'...**emotional exhaustion**...' Hall, A. T., Frink, D. D. & Buckley, M. R. (2017). An accountability account: A review and synthesis of the theoretical and empirical research on felt accountability. *Journal of Organizational Behavior, 38*(2), 204-224.

'...**and depressed mood at work**...' Zellars, K. L., Hochwarter, W. A., Lanivich, S. E., Perrewé, P. L. & Ferris, G. R. (2011). Accountability for others, perceived resources, and well-being: Convergent restricted non-linear results in two samples. *Journal of Occupational and Organizational Psychology, 84*(1), 95-115.

'**Accountability can function as both a challenge, which boosts performance, or as a threat**...' Schlenker, B. R. & Weigold, M. F. (1989). Self-identification and accountability. In R. A. Giacalone & P. Rosenfeld (Eds.), *Impression Management in the Organization* (pp. 21–43). Lawrence Erlbaum Associates, Inc.

APPENDIX: CASE STUDIES

IF WE ARE NOT AWARE, IT CAN BE EASY TO CROSS THE TIPPING point from *activated accountability* to the 'dark side' of *over-accountability* and/or *inappropriate accountability*. Contextual factors play a large part in determining the location of this tipping point. To illustrate what this could look like and how it can be addressed, the case studies that follow look at three specific accountability contexts that will influence the tipping point and demonstrate how to deal with them.

Case study 1: Asking for accountability with tired and testy teams

Accountability is what's going to make the difference in the progress and performance of individuals, teams and organisations, but it can feel tricky to do when people are low on energy and motivation. So how can we go about this important work, even with tired and testy teams?

The critical thing to remember about this type of work is to 'Think Global, Act Local'.

What does that mean?

While the 'what' is the global half of this equation – that is, a shift towards an Own It! culture – the 'how' needs to be tailored to meet the local context of each division, business unit and team. By understanding the local influencing factors, we're more likely to be successful in co-creating and communicating clear, realistic accountability expectations and in building fruitful accountability relationships that take account of where the team are at in terms of their motivation and energy.

As we do this 'localising' work, there are four contextual considerations to be aware of:

- **Individual** team-member readiness, performance, needs and preferences
- **Team** structure, dynamics, engagement and trust
- **Work** type, location, complexity and interdependency
- **Organisation** structure, business priorities and culture

Let's have a look at how each of these contextual considerations can be met to help us ask for accountability from people who feel they have little left to give.

THE CONTEXT

Nic is a senior leader in a large retail organisation that has been hit hard by the business disruption of COVID, and hasn't experienced the uptake in online trading to compensate for losses in store.

In parallel to the external uncertainty and disruption, there have been several internal restructures resulting in redundancies and three major 'transformation' initiatives that have required significant changes to processes and systems.

There is a level of change fatigue and burn out across the organisation, but results from the latest staff engagement and culture surveys show that Nic's team in particular is really struggling.

THE ACCOUNTABILITY CHALLENGE

Nic's team is business-critical to meeting the commercial targets required to secure the company's future; they need to be lifting their performance rather than falling further behind.

How can Nic ask for more from the team when they are already struggling?

THE ACCOUNTABILITY OPPORTUNITY

Rather than trying to solve the situation alone or 'protecting' the team by not sharing it with them, Nic can bring the team together to discuss the targets and explain how they fit into the bigger picture of the organisation. Nic can ask for the team's ideas and input about what might be barriers to achieving them, what could help them succeed, and what support they may need from other teams or departments to do so.

With the understanding that they may be stretch goals, Nic can also invite candid feedback about whether the team feels that any aspects of the targets are completely unrealistic, and, if so, what would need to change to make them achievable.

By the end of these discussions, Nic needs to ensure that there is clarity, understanding, and agreed commitment to what needs to be achieved; who will be responsible for what aspects of the work, how progress will be tracked, monitored and shared, and when it needs to be completed by; and the implications and consequences for the team, other departments, and the organisation as a whole if they are not met.

Nic can then check in with individual team members after the team discussion to see how they are feeling in terms of their levels of motivation and commitment to do the work ahead. This is a critical aspect of the process that many leaders miss.

Understanding team members' levels of motivation will help Nic provide the necessary and appropriate support and/or encouragement where needed. And if a team member's motivation or commitment is on the low side, then it's an opportunity for Nic to learn more about that individual by asking what it would take to improve it by just 5% or 10%.

THE RESULT

By doing what's outlined above, Nic touches on all four of the Accountability Context considerations:

- Explaining how the targets fit into the bigger picture and the implications of not meeting them speaks to the **organisational context**.
- Asking for feedback from the team about barriers, enablers and what may be unrealistic targets addresses the **work context**.
- Gaining clarity and consensus through discussions on the what, who, when, where and how of the work will define the **team context**.

- Following up with team members after the group discussion about their feelings of motivation and commitment explores the **individual context**.

We know that accountability relies on two factors: the *clarity of expectations* and *quality of accountability relationships*. And we can see in the case study above how these work together in the process that Nic implements: first, getting clear about the what, why, when, where, who and how; and then monitoring the quality of relationships with and within the team to question, clarify and call out what doesn't feel possible or realistic.

So, if you have an accountability challenge like Nic where you're being instructed to ask more of people who are physically tired, emotionally exhausted and feel that they don't have any more to give, try bringing them together to co-create a way forward that highlights the possibilities, identifies the barriers, and is grounded in reality, so that they can feel confident and committed to achieving it.

Case study 2: Accountability and bureaucracy – Ne'er the twain shall meet?

Despite research that suggests the many benefits of autonomous work environments and leadership styles to both wellbeing and performance, most workplaces are built on the bureaucratic principles of standardisation, specialisation, stratification, formalisation and routinisation.

Developed from a desire to carry out complex tasks with optimal efficiency, bureaucracy prioritises productivity over creativity, regulation over invention, and control over autonomy. In this kind of structure, power trickles down through layers of management, innovation is stifled, and decision rights are largely determined by your position on the organisation chart. Accountability is lost in the complexity of reporting lines, and the drag of bureaucracy manifests itself in inertia, stagnation and disempowerment.

The traditional models of organising and leadership embedded in bureaucracy crush creativity and stifle the accountability that organisations need to ensure purposeful progress and performance. This is a very real problem, because these 'costs' – both human and commercial – are not measured, remain largely hidden, and are therefore also unaddressed.

So what's the alternative?

While bureaucracy may be endemic, it is not inevitable. In Gary Hamel and Michele Zanini's book *Humanocracy*, the authors suggest a human-centred alternative to bureaucracy. When I interviewed Gary – a long-time faculty member of the London Business School who is recognised as one of the world's most influential business thinkers – he explained the seven principles that underpin humanocracy in practice. These are the three that I believe will most help support accountability:

GENERATE OWNERSHIP

By ensuring people have autonomy in their work rather than taking orders from others, they will feel more like they're running their own business, and the natural sense of ownership that comes from this will flow through to their mindset, attitudes and actions.

INTRODUCE MARKETS

As consumers, we understand the value of having choices about where and how we spend our money, but our organisation's internal services – such as HR and IT – often function like monopolies. Adopting a marketplace approach fosters more accountability through internal contracts between different activities, roles and teams.

BUILD COMMUNITY

To be able to do our best work, we need others at work who know us, care about us, and will provide support when we're struggling to meet expectations. When we're able to talk about this, we begin to build deep, trust-based relationships, which is not only good for us as individuals, but also for the teams and organisations we work in.

While studies across the world indicate that bureaucracy is growing, not shrinking, that growth doesn't happen without human intention and action. And it can be reversed through the same means.

I particularly loved Gary's advice during our interview: 'be an activist, not a terrorist'. You don't want (or need) to blow the system or your career up by trying to change the whole enterprise at a corporate level. Start where you are.

As an activist, you can conduct experiments right where you are by trying something different and collecting some data. You can start to 'hack' the existing management processes and systems by taking one of the principles and asking your team what you can do differently if, for example, you focused on building community, generating ownership, or introducing a marketplace approach.

I've seen, heard and experienced the feelings of helplessness and hopelessness in wanting to create change amid bureaucracy. Know that you can start from where you are and begin creating your 'island' of Own It! that we talked about in Chapter 3, and, at the same time, hold to the belief that the system will eventually follow your lead and change. Never underestimate the difference one person can make.

So how can you start where you are? What can you do to be an activist and begin to loosen the bind of bureaucracy and reset accountability with your team?

Case Study 3: Can accountability culture work with hybrid teams?

The kitchen bench is my 'new desk', workout gear my 'new work wardrobe' and helping my daughter with her Grade 8 maths my 'new brain break'.

Welcome to working from home. It was what we had to do during the COVID-19 pandemic, and it's what many people are choosing to continue to do (at least for some part of their work week) as their new work normal.

The challenge with having a hybrid and distributed workforce in which some people are at home and others on site is that the cues that help create cultural norms are diluted, patchy, or even missing completely. The banter with colleagues, the physical space of the workplace, even what's displayed on walls, are all cultural symbols that signal 'what's important and how we do things around here'.

Because that's what culture is all about. As we covered in Chapter 8, from an evolutionary perspective, cultural norms are what current knowledge tells us 'works' most successfully for the tribe to survive and thrive. Note what I said right there – what *current knowledge* tells us.

It can be easy to think of culture as something that is hard to change, but the reality is that culture is a *learning process* that uncovers what works for the tribe (your team) to successfully achieve its goals. As the tribe discovers more effective ways to 'survive and thrive', less effective cultural practices fall away and are replaced by newer ones that support the tribe to develop and grow.

The good news is that when we look at culture as a learning process through which groups organise and create behavioural norms that help them reach their goals, having hybrid work practices becomes less of a roadblock. Will things need to change? Yes, absolutely, because the previous cultural norms established when we were working together in person are no longer the most effective way to take your team towards success.

So, what could this look like for accountability?

Let's see how we can use the 'containers of culture' framework from Chapter 8 – the Four Rs of role modelling, routines, rituals and rhythms – to craft an accountability culture that will work with hybrid teams.

ROLE MODELLING

Our brains are wired for connection, which means that the learning and cultural cues we get from observing others is significant. This is particularly true for leaders, who – because of both their perceived and real power in the group – have greater influence in setting cultural norms.

Because of this, leaders need to be aware and intentional about how their interactions in meetings, one-on-ones or through email model the accountability mindset and behavioural norms they want the team to follow.

For example, openly sharing progress towards your goals – even when it's not going to plan – will create a cultural norm of transparency and safety. Doing this for non-work-related goals, such as fitness or a DIY project, creates the opportunity for deeper connections with the team and role models that the non-work side of life is relevant and of value too. And this kind of role modelling can be done in a Zoom chat as easily as a meeting room.

ROUTINES

One benefit of cultural norms is that they help us organise and coordinate to be effective and efficient as we achieve our goals. Routines – the way we get the work done together – are what help us do this in a work environment. They are the *mechanics* of the team.

Working remotely can have a real impact on motivation, as we lose the in-person contact with colleagues, the feeling of togetherness, and the relational energy that comes with it. Even if we're working on different projects, just being in the same physical space makes a difference – that's why co-working spaces have become so popular.

One way to help create that connection and energy with hybrid teams is to run virtual 'work caves' where the team come together via your virtual platform (Zoom, Teams, etc.) to work individually but concurrently on important tasks. One team member 'hosts' by deciding on the timing of each 'work sprint' and 'brain break' exercise, and holding accountability check-ins at various points throughout (and definitely at the end).

I've had personal experience of doing this, and found it does wonders for focus and motivation when you know you're going to have to share what you've achieved with the group at the end of the session!

RITUALS

If routines are about effectiveness of a group, rituals are about connectedness – that of the team members to each other, and also to the goals they are working towards. Rituals support the *dynamics* of the team.

Hybrid work practices make it more challenging for leaders to keep their finger on the pulse of team dynamics. Without the opportunity to walk around and 'feel' the energy of the whole team in one location, you need to take a more proactive and structured approach to ensure team members can voice concerns, raise issues and provide feedback.

Eco-friendly cleaning-products brand Method hold a quarterly, anonymous 'Come Clean' survey in which team members share their feedback on how the organisation is (or isn't) living its values and meeting its strategic commitments. The CEO then discusses the results and addresses where they might be falling down in a town hall.

An open forum like this with your team will encourage transparency, feedback and debate – all important for accountability – and, just as importantly, will make your people feel heard.

RHYTHMS

In terms of cultural norms, how frequently something happens sends a signal about how important it is to helping the team achieve its goals. With hybrid work, the accountability cultural cues and 'nudges' that are present in the physical work environment are seen and accessed less often by team members, which may mean leaders need to dial up the frequency of their virtual replacements.

For example, sales targets or project milestone trackers that may have been displayed on a wall in the workplace, and so could be seen at any time by everyone, could be the focus of fifteen-minute 'progress huddles' two or three times a week; one-on-ones that may have been monthly or quarterly over lunch now become a weekly twenty-minute check-in over a coffee. The key is to keep these short, focused, and with clear purpose. I think we'd all agree that we don't need to spend any more time in meetings!

The key to making accountability culture work from home is *intentionality*. Leaders cannot leave it to chance.

By seeing culture as a learning process and deliberately and explicitly using the Four Rs in new ways to create new (virtual) cultural norms for accountability, you can lead yourself and your team to thrive and succeed.

References

'**Despite research that suggests the many benefits**...' Slemp, G. R., Kern, M. L., Patrick, K. J. & Ryan, R. M. (2018). Leader autonomy support in the workplace: A meta-analytic review. *Motivation and Emotion, 42*(5), 706–724. https://doi.org/10.1007/s11031-018-9698-y

'**Gary Hamel's book,** Humanocracy...' Hamel, G. & Zanini, M. (2020). *Humanocracy: Creating Organizations as Amazing as the People Inside Them.* Harvard Business Review Press.

'**When I interviewed Gary**...' McQuaid, M. (Host). (2020, August 14). Can your workplace become more human? (#199) [Audio podcast episode]. In *Making Positive Psychology Work.* https://www.michellemcquaid.com/podcast/can-your-workplace-become-more-human-podcast-with-gary-hamel/

GLOSSARY

BASIC TERMS

Accountor and ***Accountee*** – the Accountee is the person who is accountable to the Accountor. These terms are intended to be hierarchically neutral – after all, a CEO is accountable to her staff just as they may be to her.

Accountability System – the interconnecting moving parts of a more complex whole and the processes through which these parts can be coordinated and organised. (Chapter 7)

Accountability Relationship – the *condition* where one party may, at some point, need to account to another party, or where one party may, at some point, hold itself accountable vis-à-vis another party. (Chapter 5)

Accountability Set-up – the *time* at which the Accountee and Accountor perceive, understand and negotiate accountability expectations. (Chapter 7)

Accountability Exchange – the *relationship* between Accountor and Accountee as the Accountability Task is being undertaken. (Chapters 7 & 8)

Accountability Response – the *specific situation* in which the Accountee is called to account by the Accountor. (Chapter 8)

Accountable – the person or stakeholder who is *the 'owner' of the work*, and who must provide their sign-off or approval when the task, objective or decision is complete. This person must make sure that responsibilities are assigned for all activities related to the work. There is *only one person who is accountable* – so basically, 'The buck stops here.' (Chapter 4)

Responsible – the persons or stakeholders who *do the work*. They are the ones who must complete the task or objective or make the necessary decisions. This means that, potentially, *several people can be jointly responsible* – 'The work is done here.' (Chapter 4)

TYPES OF ACCOUNTABILITY

External accountability – when individuals perceive *external accountability*, they are likely to perform behaviours mostly because of the perceived need to deliver outcomes to others. (Chapter 3)

Internal accountability – when individuals perceive *internal accountability*, the required behaviours or outcomes are aligned with their own values, beliefs and self-concept, which creates a perceived *obligation to oneself*. (Chapter 3)

Task behaviours – those behaviours that directly perform the core functions of a business or organisation. (Chapter 4)

Contextual behaviours – those behaviours that contribute to the social and psychological environment of a business or organisation. (Chapter 4)

Specific accountability – explicit, externally imposed expectations that we feel obliged to meet, but not exceed. (Chapter 4)

Generalised accountability – implicitly understood or perceived expectations that we feel obliged to meet regardless of personal 'return on investment'. (Chapter 4)

Process accountability – evaluation based on the means (*how* we get the work done), which allows for greater autonomy, learning, creativity and innovation. (Chapter 4)

Outcome accountability – evaluation based on the ends (*what* was achieved), which encourages pre-set patterns, avoidance of innovation, and anticipatory self-justification. (Chapter 4)

Formal accountability – expectations created, communicated and enforced through official channels (e.g., accountability processes and systems). (Chapter 4)

Informal accountability – expectations that derive from unwritten, socially shared expectations that are created, communicated and enforced outside official channels (e.g., team and group norms). (Chapter 4)

TERMINOLOGY

The Social perspective – suggests that Accountees protect their self-image and look to gain reward and avoid punishment in social groups through favourable evaluations by others. (Chapter 2)

The Internal perspective – suggests that, because accountability involves the expectation of a potential evaluation, it is driven by the same psychological processes as social identity and approval-seeking. (Chapter 2)

The Phenomenological perspective – proposes that accountability is a 'state of mind' rather than a 'state of affairs'. This puts the focus on the Accountee's subjective interpretations of the accountability situation they are facing, rather than the objective systems or processes of accountability employed by the organisation. (Chapter 2)

Adaptive challenges – situations in which the problem is difficult to clearly define, the solution is currently unknown, and the work needs to be achieved through innovation and influence rather than authority and power. (Chapter 3)

Technical challenges – problems that can be solved by the existing knowledge of experts and achieved through the exercise of authority and power. (Chapter 3)

State-based/trait-based – speaks to whether something is fixed and an inherent aspect of an individual (trait-based), or is changeable and influenced by the individual's environment (state-based). (Chapter 3)

Relational energy – the positive feeling and sense of increased resourcefulness experienced as a direct result of an interaction with someone else. (Chapter 5)

Barren accountability relationships – those relationships between Accountors and Accountees that are lifeless because they lack the nutrients, in the form of positive relational energy, to produce growth. (Chapter 5)

Fruitful accountability relationships – those relationships between Accountors and Accountees that are fuelled by positive relational energy. (Chapter 5)

Mindsets – mental frameworks that help us make sense of the world by simplifying and organising the information we need to process in any given moment.

Locus of control – refers to the extent to which people feel that they have control over the events that influence their lives. (Chapter 6)

MODELS AND FRAMEWORKS

The Accountability Reset Matrix – maps the quality of accountability relationships with the clarity of accountability expectations. It can help us become clearer on the cause of our current accountability challenges and help identify the actions we can take to support peak performance and progress. (Part II)

Accountability Mindsets: Them & Theirs – our attention is focused outward – we point fingers at others and focus on what we feel they 'should' be doing. (Chapter 6)

Accountability Mindsets: Me & Mine – our attention is pointed inward – we point the finger at ourselves, focusing on what *we* 'should' be doing, and the ways in which we feel we are failing. (Chapter 6)

Accountability Mindsets: Us & Ours – based in confidence, this comes from a mindset of ownership, with a focus on what we *can* do rather than what we feel we 'should' be doing. (Chapter 6)

Choice Points – help us to be intentional about who we want to be and how we want to show up by identifying points where we can move towards or away from our desired goal(s). (Chapter 6)

Drama Triangle – a model that describes the reality of day-to-day human dynamics, illustrating the destructive attitudes that people can take on when personal responsibility and power come into conflict. (Chapter 8)

Progress Triangle – the antidote to the Drama Triangle, this model is composed of three constructive attitudes that people can take on to encourage and accept personal responsibility. (Chapter 8)

Learning Loop – helps you to identify the learnings that can be derived from previous actions, and apply them to future efforts to ensure continual improvement. (Chapter 8)

Four Rs – four containers that have a dynamic and reinforcing relationship with each other, which makes them the most effective variables to work with when seeking to create change in a cultural system. (Chapter 9)

Behaviour Change Loop – a framework to intentionally design behaviour change that taps into the way our brains are naturally wired to create change. (Chapter 9)

SCARF model – a tool for understanding what can trigger a threat/avoidance response. (Chapter 2)

Six Ws – the six basic questions (Who, What, When, Where, Why and How) that provide a useful 'checklist' to help ensure that accountability expectations are looked at from a number of different perspectives. (Chapter 4)

WANT MORE?

IF YOU'RE LOOKING TO CREATE AN EXPERIENCE THAT EMPOWERS people to lead through disruption and uncertainty with confidence and clarity, look no further.

Offering practical evidence-based strategies they can immediately apply, Dr Paige Williams combines playful humour with a meaningful message, streetwise smarts with evidence-based data, and delivers it in a way that feels like dinner-table conversation.

Whether on a conference stage or in a lecture theatre or board room, Paige leaves people with the confidence and motivation they need to succeed.

Find out more at drpaigewilliams.com.